A
BLACK
POLITICAL
THEOLOGY

Books by J. Deotis Roberts
Published by The Westminster Press

A Black Political Theology

Liberation and Reconciliation:
A Black Theology

A
BLACK
POLITICAL
THEOLOGY

by J. Deotis Roberts

THE WESTMINSTER PRESS
PHILADELPHIA

PUBLISHED BY THE WESTMINSTER PRESS ®
PHILADELPHIA, PENNSYLVANIA

PRINTED IN THE UNITED STATES OF AMERICA

Library of Congress Cataloging in Publication Data

Roberts, James Deotis.
    A black political theology.

    Includes bibliographical references.
    1. Theology, Doctrinal. 2. Negroes—Religion.
I. Title.
BT75.2.R6   230   74-4384
ISBN 0-664-24988-4

For My Parents

Let your motto be resistance! *resistance! resistance!* No oppressed people have ever secured their liberty without resistance. What kind of resistance you had better make, you must decide by circumstances that surround you, and according to the suggestion of expediency. Brethren, adieu! Trust in the living God. Labor for the peace of the human race, and remember that you are *four millions.—Henry Highland Garnet, Buffalo, N.Y., 1843; in Earl Ofari,* The Life and Thought of Henry Highland Garnet *(Beacon Press, 1972), p. 153.*

Bring no more vain oblations; incense is an abomination unto me; the new moons and sabbaths, the calling of assemblies, I cannot away with; it is iniquity, even the solemn meeting.

Wash ye, make you clean; put away the evil of your doings from before mine eyes; cease to do evil; learn to do well; seek judgment, relieve the oppressed, judge the fatherless, plead for the widow.—*Isa. 1:13, 16–17(KJV).*

Take thou away from me the noise of thy songs; for I will not hear the melody of thy viols. But let judgment run down as waters, and righteousness as a mighty stream.—*Amos 5:23–24(KJV).*

Contents

Acknowledgments

The present volume is a continuation of my previous writings on black theology. I am indebted to my students at the School of Religion, Howard University; at the College of Arts and Sciences of the Catholic University of America; and at George Mason College of the University of Virginia; and to all those church and academic groups throughout the nation with whom I have discussed the subject matter of this volume. The Howard University faculty research program under the able direction of Dr. Andrew Billingsley, Vice-President for Academic Affairs, has been generous in funding my research during the past several years.

The staff of The Westminster Press has encouraged me all along the way. Mrs. Sylvia Hecht has again labored long hours to type this manuscript. Without the love and confidence of my wife and children, I would not have had the peace of mind to complete this task.

J. D. R.

School of Theology
Virginia Union University
Richmond, Virginia

Introduction

A book should have a perspective. The present work is a constructive attempt at theological interpretation within the perspective of black awareness. Many peoples today have a new consciousness. The writer is avowedly *black*. The reader will note that the theological positions of neo-orthodoxy and the British postliberal theologians have shaped my thought. I have been aided in my thinking by existentialism and the theology of hope. To be honest, it would be well for me to mention how much classical Western philosophy and theology have impinged upon my mind and spirit. My study of Christian Platonism will always be in focus. The study of Eastern and African religions will be reflected from time to time, but I want to speak from the Christian faith claim in its healing and social dimensions. My purpose is to speak to the whole man, body and spirit, in solitude and in the encounter with other persons-in-community.

For most thoughtful Americans Vietnam and Watergate—a tragedy abroad and a scandal at home—symbolize the "conscienceless power" aspect of American life. Racism in the experience of blacks has been and remains the cancer of this society. The recent decisions of the "Nixon Court" indicate the extent to which the "separation of powers" doctrine of the Founding Fathers has been transgressed. The Martin Luther King era of nonviolent protest has been brought to a close. This was a period when law and morality were combined in the interest of civil rights. But blacks in their struggle for liberation can no longer rely on the liberal civil rights decisions of a "Warren Court" or the moral leadership of a John F. Kennedy. There is ample evidence that America has lost its conscience and is now in danger of losing its soul. Even Jeane Dixon, a pro-Establishment forecaster of good news for the Nixon administration, has warned that Americans must unite or prepare for the worst. A more truthful prophecy would be a message of judgment and repentance beginning at the White House.

At a time when we might refer prophetically to the decline and fall of America, one wonders why the pulpit is so silent. One longs for those sermons not suitable to be preached in the White House. In this period when "conscienceless power confronts a powerless conscience," the call for a theological ethic in black perspective is imperative. There is evidence that Dr. King's dream has been deferred. But, even more disturbing, there is evidence of corruption in high places, repression of minorities and a phasing out of humane programs—all this at a time when the Pentagon never had it so good. We have become a nation of bandits at home and abroad, operating beyond the laws of man and God.

Law and order without justice will not save us. "Peace

with honor" based upon a policy of "bomb and negotiate" will not save us. "God and country" based upon the principle "My country, right or wrong," will not save America. Nothing short of collective repentance can save us as a people now. We require a confession of our national sins and a transvaluation of our values—from greed and lust for power with which to dehumanize the black and the poor, to a lack of concern for making life more human for all. Programs to make life "sweeter for those who are already doing well" will not redeem this nation. White House sermons by conservative preachers who have a vested interest in affluence and who preach a *status quo* gospel will not suffice. The Protestant ethic undergirded by a bootstrap philosophy will not aid the oppressed who are without boots. A personal piety without a public ethic will not redeem our land. The gospel à la Billy Graham cannot purge America of its collective sin and guilt at home and abroad. We are in need of social salvation as well as personal salvation. We need to be saved as a people, as a nation.

There is a need for a theology growing out of the experience of the *black American*. Whereas today there is much excitement over a revolutionary theology in general, and a theology of hope in particular, the unique problems of the black experience are not properly treated. Most of the theologies of hope, liberation, and revolution center in the Marxist-Christian dialogue in Europe, in liberation struggles in southern Africa, or in the political upheavals in Latin America. While black Americans share the aspirations of others in the Third World, they are constantly reminded of Dr. King's prophecy: "All Africa will be free

before black Americans are free." Many of these programs
in political theology are highly theoretical, ivory-tower
pursuits indulged in by those far removed by race and
space from the fray. There is an obvious need for empirical programs *by* and *for* those engaged in the struggle for
liberation.

In the "land of the free and the home of the brave," we
are called upon as black theologians to speak out of the
sufferings and experiences of oppression of black Americans for whom the promise of "freedom and justice for
all" has not been kept. It is not the duty of a black theologian to speak for all "minorities" and "ethnics." He
should encourage these to speak for themselves, loud and
clear, until they are heard. They alone know the depths of
their sufferings and their hunger for liberation. While I
have a compassionate empathy for all oppressed people
at home and abroad, my task is to interpret the faith in
order that my people may be set free from the bondage
created and sustained by white racism. I fear that by speaking for *all,* I will not be able to speak for *any.* The white
oppressor must be confronted by the scandal of particularity. He must not be allowed the escape hatch of universality.

Existing programs in political theology do raise important issues for black theologians. The issues, insights,
methods of discourse, and ethical principles of some of
these programs will aid the black theologian as he interprets the faith in the light of the black experience. Furthermore, significant dialogue is beginning between black and
white theologians in the form of articles and essays. Frederick Herzog has provided us with a book on *Liberation
Theology* (1972). Herzog has been in conversation with

James Cone and he attempts to "think black." However, in America, thinking black and being black are poles apart. This is why black theologians must continue to do their own thing.[1]

I

Foundations

Theology is *reasoned* interpretation of the intellectual content of the Christian faith. This is an aspect of theology which is satisfying to the mind. Theology is a reflection upon experience as well. This is the approach to theology which moves the heart and will. Theology is "God-talk," *logos* about *theos,* or talking and reasoning about God.

Theology has to do with divine revelation. It is not based upon a human quest for God. We have been found by God. God's approach to man is the basis of our spiritual quest. His finding us is the motive behind our seeking him. Theology involves our reflection upon the divine-human personal encounter. Theology interprets a redemptive drama in which God and man are involved on the plane of history.

Jesus Christ is the norm of the Christian revelation, but he is not the limit. God has not left himself without witness at any place or time. God's revelation to man spans all space and all time; it moves through all creation and all history. A narrow Christocentric view of revelation that distinguishes between religion and the Christian faith is unworthy. It is obviously inadequate for a theological program that traces its heritage to the Third World.

James Cone will need to break with Barthianism if he is to enter into meaningful dialogue with African theologians who are taking seriously their precolonial religious traditions.[1] And all black theology must take ethnocentricity seriously in order to treat the particularity of the black experience with antecedents in Africa. We will need to understand the meaning of religion and the revelation of God so as not to see a conflict between God's revelation to peoples of Africa and his revelation in Jesus Christ. But this does not mean that God's revelation in Christ is no longer the norm for all authentic Christian revelation. Indeed, God's revelation in Christ is the key that unlocks the meaning of all revelation.

Thus Cone's outline of the meaning of revelation—which he considers to be one of his strongest points—turns out to be a most inadequate position. Black theology requires an understanding of revelation sufficiently comprehensive to deal with the pan-African context of the black religious experience. The Christocentric view of revelation drawn ready-made from Barth will not foster the transatlantic conversation between black American and African theologians who together are seeking a decolonized expression of theology. What would be helpful is an understanding of the revelation of God as manifest in all creation and all history as measured by the supreme revelation of God in the incarnation. Archbishop William Temple's classic statement on revelation is worth repeating here:

> Unless all existence is a medium of revelation, no particular revelation is possible. . . . Either all occurrences

are in some degree revelation of God, or else there is no such revelation at all; for the conditions of the possibility of any revelation require that there should be nothing which is not revelation. Only if God is revealed in the rising of the sun in the sky can He be revealed in the rising of the Son of man from the dead.[2]

Charles H. Long has the promise of providing the meaning and context for the total African and Afro-American religious experience. His appreciation for religion is worldwide. But unfortunately his interest is almost completely anthropological, historical, and phenomenological.[3] There is a lack of interest in religion as conviction and commitment—the cornerstone of theological construction. This means that Long's writings do not provide a needed corrective for Cone's Barthian understanding of revelation. Both divine revelation and human religion—with commitment—are needed as the proper basis for a theology to span the pan-African religious experience.

What is the meaning of "black" in black theology? Words communicate meanings. This should be clearly borne in mind when we encounter the word "black" here. It is true that Afro-Americans have called themselves by many names. This reflects the identity crisis through which we have been moving in reference to our personhood and our peoplehood. We have called ourselves "African," "colored," "Negro," "Afro-American," and now "black." The fact that we, or at least some of us, call ourselves black today may indicate that this crisis sponsored and sustained by white racism is continuous.

Some may ask: What's in a name? The answer: a great deal if the name conveys meaning. "Black" is a symbol of self-affirmation. Some blacks wish to dismiss the meaning of "black" by recalling how most blacks would have rejected the name a few years ago. The fact that many use the word with a sense of dignity and pride does not convince these blacks that the word has positive content. They are locked in the old mind-set and refuse to "think black."

It is true that dictionary definitions of "black" include words such as "wicked," "disastrous," and "hostile." Definitions of "white" include "innocent," "fortunate," and "decent." Color takes on both aesthetic and ethical meaning. Black is considered ugly and bad; white is considered beautiful and good. Speaking in racist terms, the bearer of black skin is inferior, while the bearer of white skin is superior.

The affirmation of blackness may mean that we have rejected these traditional definitions. In so doing we have rejected the image of black that exists in the white mind. We have redefined the term "black." We have decolonized our mind and we have transvalued our aesthetic and ethical values in reference to the meaning of the word "black." We have redefined the term "black." We are black and proud. Black is beautiful. We find in this new outlook a basis for a pride of heritage and for the dignity of our person.

We have also redefined "white" to the point that we no longer accept whiteness as an indication of goodness, beauty, or purity. We accept whites as equals but not as superiors. We can now—as Martin Luther King, Jr., put it—judge people by the content of their character rather than by the complexion of their skin. We no longer allow white racists to define our being or cause us to hate our people and ourselves. This is a positive step forward in a new self-understanding that enables us to experience psy-

chological liberation. This understanding of "black" has
great importance for developing a black theology.

While in Atlanta during June, 1973, a group of black
scholars in religion paid a visit to Ebenezer Baptist Church.
We viewed the grave site of Martin Luther King, Jr., and
then entered the church, where we were greeted by Martin
Luther King, Sr., affectionately referred to as Daddy King.
In the course of our conversation the word "black" came
up. We were involved in a workshop session in the Society
for the Study of Black Religion. Daddy King immediately
informed us that he was not black. Looking us straight in
the eyes, he asked: "Are you black?" One brave brother
among us said frankly but politely: "Yes, sir!" We were
all shocked by the challenge but shared the experience
with the larger fellowship. Whereas we all were united on
the terms of black awareness, we realized that Daddy King
represents a large segment of powerful black churchmen
for whom black theology has no real meaning.

I can recall a lecture that I presented to a local church
of middle-class blacks. My lecture was to be the basis for
a day's discussion. I was reminded by those present that
if the word "black" had not been used in the announce-
ment of my lecture title more people would have been
present. Indeed, several persons present missed the content
of my lecture, being completely engrossed in getting me to
drop the word "black." They considered my message
worthy, but they saw the word "black" as a real disad-
vantage.

For many people of African descent, "Afro-American"
or "African-American" may in the long run say the same
thing that we are conveying by the term "black." There are
many blacks who are not able to redefine "black"; nor are

they able to accept any meaning of the term other than that provided by white authorities. When the word is used by other blacks, they are turned off, disassociate themselves from this usage, and are unable to distinguish between the medium and the message.

For the present, however, "black" says a great deal that needs saying. We are not considered, nor are we treated, as most hyphenated Americans. In a country that promises freedom, equality, and justice for all, we are a huge minority that has not melted. There is something profoundly meaningful in taking a term filled with shame and placing upon it a halo of glory. This has great ethical and theological import. There is even something Christlike in taking something shameful in the eyes of the white oppressor and investing it with pride and dignity. The cross, despised by Jews and Romans alike as a symbol of utter rejection, is for Christians a glorious symbol of God's matchless love. "Black," therefore, in the reconception of black theology, is a meaningful symbol of our new self-understanding as persons in black skin who are equal in nature and grace with all humans.

The context in which the Christian faith is to be understood today is highly political. A new consciousness or sensibility is upon us that has to do with humanizing structures of power. What H. Richard Niebuhr taught us about the social sources of denominationalism now has to be learned about the political location of theology. In general in this country a new privatization of religious experience or an overwhelming concern for the inner life is coming to the surface. Religion is the new "old-time" religion. Emphasis is shifting from transforming or saving society to a state of soul or personal relationship with Christ. We have a blend of Eastern mysticism, American spiritualism, and the success syndrome. Churches are revitalized by speaking in tongues, by an outpouring of the gifts of the Spirit, by a rebirth of Pentecostalism, Satanism, astrology, astral projection, and witchcraft. Trust in our technological utopia has been shattered by a sense of emptiness. Thus white Americans, including the young who formerly protested against war and racism, have fallen back on the individual experience of God, which has deep roots in American Christianity.

The Puritan ethic is translated into the principle of capitalist exploitation of the oppressed. If you are not successful in business or politics, you are not really trusting in God; hence you get the Full Gospel Business Men's movement with its emphasis on the outpouring of the Holy Spirit and tongues of fire. There is little indication that theology is seen as a socially directed and action-oriented enterprise. This is against the grain of the prevailing individualism in present-day theology characterized by the Protestant work ethic, the phasing out of poverty programs, and corruption in high places. In the social field we have not won a peace with honor, yet God and country, law and order, are accompanied by piety on the Potomac and White House sermons.

The fact that racism has not been overcome means that blacks cannot afford to be faddists and cop out of the struggle for their humanity and their liberation. The tired liberals are suffering from a societal fatigue and have turned within themselves. But we have had Jesusology and heavenly promises all these years, and we dare not become Jesus freaks at a time when we are involved in a militant thrust to humanize life for the black and the poor in the present life. We cannot rest in a private and intense religious experience that does not lead us to public action against oppressed structures of power. A privatized, quietistic version of theology is inadequate for the oppressed. What we need is a political theology—a theology of power.

We shall not abandon the quest for the strengthening of the inner life, for this is deep in our psyche and heritage. At the same time we are anxious to know what God is doing in all creation and history as well as in ourselves. Evangelism among blacks must be more than telling the old, old story. Without our deeds of caring and giving, our telling is mere verbiage, "full of sound and fury, signifying nothing."

The perspective of black theology is being sharpened by the "liberation theology" of Latin America, which is different from the theology of hope as set forth by Moltmann and Pannenberg. The assumptions of European and American theologians about how God relates to humans differ from those of Rubem Alves of Brazil and Gustavo Gutiérrez of Peru. Moltmann and Pannenberg are speaking out of affluent and serene ivory towers, even though they try hard to be sensitive to poverty and oppression. Likewise, there is a difference between hope and liberation in Carl Braaten, Frederick Herzog, and Rosemary Ruether. While the latter two can speak of "thinking black" with some real empathy derived from involvement with oppressed groups, they do not bear for a lifetime the "mark of oppression." Being white they can take up and lay down the burden of oppression at will. The black theologian, on the other hand, knows what it means to bear the "mark of Cain" for a lifetime. There is even a very important experiential difference between those black theologians who speak from the ivory towers of white academic centers in the North and those who identify with the poverty and insecurity of struggling black academic institutions in the South. How ironical it is that those black scholars in religion who have set themselves up as kingmakers and the chief spokesmen of black religious experience are part of the "brain drain" and choose not to suffer the afflictions of their people. Latin-American theologians, on the other hand, labor and suffer with the oppressed. Their theology is from authority, the authority of experience, rather than from authorities.

Latin theologians have a deep empathy and identification with the oppressed masses. Whereas Euro-American theologians speak "from authorities" concerning the oppressed, Alves, Gutiérrez, Paulo Freire and Dom Helder Camara speak with the authority of experience. It is at this point that black theologians and their African brothers in southern Africa join the oppressed in Latin America as those who belong to a fellowship that bears the mark of pain. All these theologians are done with a cautious, gradualistic approach to the humanization of life. We all belong to a long-suffering people. The gospel suitable for this new consciousness is one that opts for radical and massive change in oppressive social attitudes and structures of power.

The definitions of Paulo Freire in his major work could almost be appropriated by black theologians.[4] The oppressed feel themselves to be objects owned by someone else, emotionally dependent upon the "boss," the one who imposes values upon them. This leads to a self-depreciation that becomes a pattern of hopelessness about doing anything to change their condition. The oppressor is characterized by a will to dominate or to subject everyone and everything to his purchasing power, and he is determined to use technology as a means of manipulating the oppressed. This pathological condition is characteristic of white racism. Freire is just as accurate as he turns to a cure. He describes "conscientization" as a continuous process of forming a consciousness of one's own human worth and future possibilities as well as a critical awareness of the ways one exploits himself and others. "Conscientization" offers an insightful way for reappropriating and reinterpreting the Biblical message of salvation through honest confession, repentance (*metanoia*), and rebirth, as God enables us to be reborn in new relationships. What better models could black theologians adopt for their message of liberation to the black oppressed masses?

The exodus is interpreted by Gutiérrez as paradigmatic of God's manner of acting in history and throughout creation.[5] In the light of this event, the creator and liberator of Israel is affirmed as the creator of the world and the Lord of history. Creation was the first salvific act, and salvation continues as a liberating, re-creating, and fulfilling activity. The kingdom of love, justice, and peace is being partially fulfilled throughout history. The Parousia is necessarily and inevitably historical, temporal, earthly, social, and material. To work to transform the world is also to save. To struggle against misery and exploitation and to build a just social order is already to be part of the saving action, which is moving toward complete fulfillment. This is to take part in God's saving process, which includes the whole man and all of history. Faith is manifest in social praxis. In this way the prophetic and the pastoral interests of theology are united. In these as in other penetrating insights Gutiérrez offers sound foundational principles that black theologians should ponder with all seriousness.

Indigenization is a key concept for black theology as it is for all socially conscious programs in theology. There have been several attempts to indigenize theology in recent years. This process is essential whenever theology becomes more than an exercise that is rational and abstract. This is true when theology touches upon religious existentialist affections, as found in the writings of Richard R. Niebuhr, who is fascinated with Jonathan Edwards and Friedrich Schleiermacher. His recent work entitled *Experiential Religion* [6] is an attempt at a mature and creative expression of his outlook. John E. Smith in *Experience and God* takes a similar position. These are recent attempts at religious and theological interpretations that have characterized much essential theologizing from the beginning. The Boston personalistic school, which influenced Martin Luther King Jr., was based upon a radical empiricism. The point is made. Much theology in general and existentialism in particular has taken experience seriously. Whenever this occurs, something of the theologian and his social situation radiates through his message.

What we have in mind when we refer to "indigenization" is more ambitious and conscious. It is a deliberate and avowed acceptance of "context" or "situation" as the matrix of theological discourse. An indigenized theology takes us beyond the so-called national theologies of the past and the present. It is not in the same category as a "German," "Swedish," or "British" theology. Herbert W. Richardson's "American theology" is "American," but it is also "Western." All such programs, including the "death of God" theologies, claim universality, but they are in fact Euro-American. They are based upon the assumption of a social Darwinism that places Western man —his thought, religion, and culture—at the pivot. For the most part these programs aim at logical precision more than they do at ethical decision and social change.

The black theologian must turn to the Third World, to Latin America, to Asia and Africa, to observe theological models of "indigenization" worthy of his consideration. We have already referred to what some Latin-American theologians are doing to indigenize theology. E. Bolaji Idowu, a minister and a professor of religious studies at the University of Ibadan, Nigeria, writes concerning indigenization, using the following pointed illustration:

> In 1956, I took part as an assistant missioner in a Mission to the University College, Ibadan. The Chief Missioner, who was an American, used some American films based upon the Gospel narratives to introduce the subtheme for each evening. The first film startled me; the rest of the films left me disturbed; and they set me thinking deeply. . . . According to the films, Jesus Christ was speaking American. . . . I suddenly realized that all along, the picture of Jesus Christ which I had in mind was that of an English person speaking in correct English idiom and accent. It did not really occur to me that Jesus Christ was capable of speaking American! This showed that all along, I had seen Him only through the eyes of my English educators; and similarly, a Nigerian whose Christian education had been conducted by an American or a Swedish Missionary, for example, would see through the eyes of his educator an American or a Swedish Jesus! [7]

According to Idowu, the church in Nigeria should bear the unmistakable stamp of that country and affirm the

Lordship of Jesus Christ rather than remain a colony of human overlords from England or America. Nigerian Christians must now be allowed to hear the voice of Jesus Christ and interpret his will for themselves.[8] The thought is that of a Nigerian, but the mood is that of many blacks in America today.

Raymond Panikkar was brought up in a Hindu-Catholic environment. He studied the Hindu scriptures and philosophy alongside the Bible. He also studied Western philosophy and theology in several European countries. He argues that Hindu philosophy should find its place in Christian thought in the same way that Plato and Aristotle found their place in Christian theology. Panikkar maintains that Hindu philosophy is in reality more in agreement with Christianity than is Aristotelian philosophy. This is indeed a bold assertion for a Catholic priest-scholar to make. Was not Aristotle accepted by "the Angelic Doctor," Thomas Aquinas, as the philosopher par excellence? Panikkar sees Christ already at work in Hinduism, and he declares that the good Hindu is saved by the sacraments of Hinduism. According to him, the Hindu view of the Absolute and the Lord foreshadows the Christian doctrine of the Trinity. He goes so far as to make this bold assertion:

> A Christian will never "understand" Hinduism if he is not converted to Hinduism. Never will a Hindu "understand" Christianity unless he becomes a Christian.[9]

Western Christians have great difficulty understanding what Panikkar is talking about. But when I heard Indian theologians speak of the *Vedas* as their Old Testament, or of Sanskrit rather than Hebrew as a Biblical language, it was not difficult for me to interpret their meaning. The black theologian can understand, for he is about a similar task.

There are indigenizing programs developing around the world, but my final illustration comes from the Far East. A recent issue of the *Northeast Asia Journal of Theology* (March, 1973) contains a book review that makes the point.[10] Sun Hwan Pyun reviews the book by Sung Bum Yan entitled *The Korean Theology: A Yellow Theology* (Seoul: Sun Myung Moon Wha Sha, 1972). The reviewer heralds this work as an innovation that is part of a process of "de-Westernization" during the postcolonial era. He compares this Korean work of "indigenized theology" with James H. Cone's *A Black Theology of Liberation* and Panikkar's work, discussed above.

Professor Yan (of the Methodist Theological Seminary in Seoul) studied at Basel under Karl Barth. He also studied at Doshisha University in Kyoto, Japan. He uses the Confucian concept of "sincerity" as a hermeneutical tool in the same manner in which Barth used "the word of God." His goal is to understand the situation of Korea more adequately and to seek contacts between the Christian gospel and the culture and religions of Korea. He is rebelling against the "colonial subordination of thought" and the Western "Babylonian captivity of theology." He chooses the theory of syncretism rather than the theory of transformation of culture. "Sincerity" is a principle of harmony between heaven, earth, and men. The Western principle is "contrast." In ethics, Yan views the Confucian family-centered ethic as a possible way to correct the self-centered individual ethics of the West. It is his view that this "yellow theology" can provide for Koreans a "living theology." On the one hand it can provide a Christian understanding of present reality, and on the other hand it provides a perspective for new historical realities to unfold.

What has come through in this brief survey of indigenized theology is a new awareness that is widespread in the Third World. Christian theologians are attempting to decolonize theology and make it speak more meaningfully out of the culture and the history of the people for whom the faith is interpreted. This is a vital process if theology is to be more than "dry bones" for faith. The masses of people in these parts of the world are among the "wretched of the earth." They have much in common with the black poor in this country, who live a precarious existence. It is not difficult, therefore, to understand the mutual interest now developing among the theologians of the Third World.

When the black theologians began their task, there was no time to consider the question of method. The message they had was "like fire shut up in their bones." In the words of Mordecai Johnson, "It was too hot for paper." The word they had to set forth was agonizing in birth pains to be delivered. The "King of love" was dead. There were the "long, hot summers," and "benign neglect" was urged as the national policy on racial problems. Methodology per se has to be considered in a calm, reflective climate. It is not the product of troubled waters. Black theologians were not permitted the luxury of becoming methodological experts. Furthermore, their message was different. They needed new ways of thinking and entering into theological discourse.

Another reason why the question of method did not seriously claim our attention was that this issue does not impress itself upon all theologians with the same urgency. It happened that the pioneers in black theology were not method men. Indeed, if one examines theology in general, he will find that only a few theologians are preoccupied with the question of method. For most theologians, method is only a means to get things done, and there may be several ways to get things done, however imperfectly.

It is interesting to observe that some theologians who have made a real contribution to method did so after writing major theological documents. On the other hand, there are those whose initial contribution to theology is a method of theological discourse. We cannot gainsay the importance of such a theological program. All theology is aided by methodological precision. As more black theologians enter the discussion, some will concentrate on the question of method. William Jones of Yale Divinity School is emerging as a black theologian who will pursue relentlessly the question of method.[11] He is giving method primary consideration and is indicating at least the direction a method for theological discourse might take. The work of William Jones should be followed with great interest, for through his criticisms we have been challenged to be more precise in our methodological considerations. His work also indicates that black theologians are not and should not be of the same persuasion. There is unity-in-diversity among us. This must continue if we are not to stifle creativity and abort our constructive task. Whereas some outsiders indicate a need for a monolithic black theology, I am pleased to report that this narrow view does not exist among black theologians themselves.[12] We are aware that ours is a theology in the making. We desire to participate in the process and give direction and encouragement to others just undertaking the task.

Theology must be horizontal as well as vertical. Walter Capps writes concerning the "two religions" of Christianity.[13] His purpose is to draw a line between religion that operates between man and man and religion that is mainly concerned about man's relation to God. On the ethical front, the difference is that between an active humanism, on one hand, and a quietistic transcendence, on the other. Again it has to do with a distinction made by Johannes Metz between a faith for community and the "privatization" of faith.

These two views are not mutually exclusive, but there is a clear difference in the direction of focus. The first is horizontal, while the second is vertical. Western theology, whether European or American, seems somehow at a loss to overcome the dualism in thought introduced by Plato. It is for this reason that the theologians of hope feel that they must denounce existential theology in view of its overemphasis upon the "I-Thou" formula in faith and ethics. They would erect a political theology upon the ruins of the introspective theology of existence. Unfortunately, most theologians see their task as either that of sacralizing the secular or secularizing the sacred. The "death of God" theologians, through a loss of transcendence and an attempt to establish a "Christian atheism," undertook to secularize the sacred. The theologians of hope, as theologians of the Word who advocate the "triumph of grace" reminiscent of Barth's program, are attempting to sacralize the secular.

The intention of this study is to present what may be called a "third religion" of Christianity. There is a need for an understanding of the Christian faith which avoids

these extremes but which provides a synthesis of the sacred
and the secular, the priestly and the prophetic dimensions
of the Christian faith. Faith and ethics are joined in what
we are calling *a black political theology*.

Joseph Washington, Jr., in his *Black Religion* (1964),
added a "fourth religion" to the three major American
"religions" discussed by Will Herberg in his *Protestant—
Catholic—Jew* (1955). Washington correctly pointed to
the omission of the black religious heritage in American
religious studies. It is important to look at the broader
black religious heritage in order to be informed concerning
the manner in which blacks have appropriated the Christian faith. Thus, this insight of Washington is helpful to
black theologians who must take this heritage with all
seriousness. The black theologian, however, must be more
than a sociologist or historian of black religion. He is an
interpreter of the Christian faith to which he is committed.
Therefore the concept of a "third religion" of Christianity
seems suggestive of what we are after here. Using the hori-
zontal-vertical typology of Capps, we shall attempt to
provide the basis upon which the sacred and the secular
dimensions of faith and ethics may be merged. It should
be remembered, however, that any method used in this
study will serve a purpose and is provisional to that end.
We are asserting boldly that black theology is a theological
ethic.

The authority for theology is rooted in the Bible, which
bears witness to God's supreme self-unveiling in Jesus
Christ. The Bible, however, is a very human book revealing
the weaknesses and the ignorance of the men who penned
it as authors and redactors. The books of the Bible bear
witness to the light, but they are not the light or the life

that breaks forth into history in the incarnate Lord. The Bible is a source book for theology, but it must be interpreted under the guidance of the Holy Spirit, who leads us into truth. As we read the Bible, it is the Spirit that broods over the chaos of our minds and spirits to teach, illumine, and guide. In the study of the Bible we must be open to what God says to us through this record. The Bible as a source for theology is to be taken seriously but not literally. God speaks through the words of the Bible, but Jesus is the Word who enlightens us concerning these words.

The Bible is a book well loved in the black community and the black church. Black saints and sinners alike quote from its pages. It is a religious textbook for blacks. Even Black Muslims quote from the Bible more than they do from the Koran. Does this indicate that they are Christian heretics rather than Islamic sectaries? At any rate, the Bible has made an unusual impression upon "the souls of black folk." This is a very good reason why the black theologian should *reread* the Bible. The Bible has been misread *by* blacks and *to* blacks. It was first misread to them by white preachers. It has also been misread by black preachers. White preachers read the opiate passages to blacks to make them "satisfied slaves" and "docile servants." Many black preachers read "survival" passages to blacks to keep them submissive and to provide sedatives for the pain and the suffering caused by racism. Add to this the escapist pie-in-the-sky interpretation of the Bible and it becomes clear why young, progressive blacks cannot buy this version of the Bible or the theology associated with it.

There are good reasons, then, why the Bible should be reread. There is a *feel* for the Bible in the hearts and lives of blacks. The Bible goes to the center of the black religious experience. This is especially true of the exodus, the prophets, and Jesus. Carter G. Woodson made a valid point when he asserted that the black man has an "oriental mind." This explains why the illiterate black slave understood the Bible better than the learned white preacher or missionary who taught him. The Bible has a lot to say about justice, love, and mercy, about liberation from oppression, about deliverance from bondage, and about making life human. The privileged need definitions, rationalizations, logical conviction, and language clarity to understand liberation, justice, and mercy. The oppressed have an immediate and intuitive understanding of such things. A black man reared in this society does not need a constitutional lawyer or a logic professor to explain "justice" or "injustice" to him. From early childhood the meanings of the words are apparent. Thus, when the Bible speaks of love, justice, and mercy, its message goes right to the soul of the black man.

In this time of black consciousness, the black man who rereads the Bible will be greatly rewarded. Its message to the black man is personal and social. The Bible speaks existentially to the individual black man, but it also addresses black people. For example, the bondage of Israel becomes their bondage and the deliverance of Israel their deliverance. When we reread the Bible, notwithstanding Paul's conservatism, we discover that the Bible holds to a "holistic" view of man. Biblical anthropology conceives of man as a unified being—body, mind, and spirit. It follows that there is no way for an enslaved man to be free. The faulty theology—written into law—which asserted that a slave would remain chained in body and free in spirit is to be condemned as a demonic distortion of the Biblical message. Much paternalism practiced by white would-be Christians in evangelical zeal and parading as home missions among blacks, reds, and browns in this country is informed by the same bogus theology. Black people, Spanish Americans, American Indians, and Orientals are still the "heathen" near at hand for the missionary who did not get off to a foreign field. Thus the black theologian, with the aid of black Scripture specialists, must exegete and interpret the Bible in the context of the black religious experience.

Creeds and councils are also authorities for theology. These put us in touch with the traditions of our faith. But these are to be honored and not worshiped. They have historical and group significance. It is through creeds and councils that we remember our past and participate in the communion of the saints at all times and in all places. We root our faith in the Christian heritage and participate in the mind of the church as it reflects theologically upon what we as Christians believe. A black theology, insofar as it is Christian, must share in this tradition. But it need not, indeed it cannot, be time-bound or culture-bound by traditionalism if it is to be an indigenized and living theology. While it accepts what is worthy in tradition, it must reject those frozen dogmas which do not represent the living Word of God. We must be sufficiently free from the form of doctrines to grasp the content or the *esse* of the Christian faith. The black theologian must then appropriate the heart of the message and adapt it toward a message of deliverance for an oppressed and suffering people.

Bishop Joseph A. Johnson speaks of "detheologizing" the faith. He is using Bultmann's example of "demythologizing" the New Testament. (I prefer Norman Pittenger's "reconception" principle.) Bishop Johnson, a black New Testament scholar, noted preacher, and churchman, is doing a worthy job in the reinterpretation of the Christian faith in the light of the black religious experience. He is a black priest-scholar who has found his field of service as a bishop in the Christian Methodist Episcopal Church in the heart of the black belt. The concept of detheologizing is too negative for my intention. While Johnson's program is quite positive, in my understanding the concept does not cover what he is doing. The process of detheologizing fits more what James Cone was doing until his *The Spirituals and the Blues*. Black theology must not be a simple reaction to white oppression. It is rightly interested in the misinterpretations and the omissions of "white theology," which have often provided justification for the oppression of blacks, but it is considerably more than this. It is most of all constructive "reconception" of the Christian faith. Just as Pittenger is busy reconceiving the faith in the light of process philosophy, the black theologian has the task of taking seriously the faith and experience of his black fathers and the black masses.

"Life is real, life is earnest" for the black man. Religion is an experience of meaning. It provides the "courage to be" in the midst of an existence that is "threatened." It provides resources for social and psychological survival. Black Protestants find most theological programs alien to their experience. These theologies are usually more Teutonic than Anglo-Saxon and do not even consider the African heritage. Black Catholics are confronted with the even stranger Roman theological system. On the whole, German theology still dominates the thinking of American theologians. Someone has observed that the "death of God" theologians were saying what we need is love, until the Germans said what we need is hope—and perhaps what we really need is faith. A noted American historian has remarked that German philosophies come to this country to die. The same may be said of theologies. What I am suggesting is that there is a lot of theological thinking going on in this country that is not native to our needs and experience. Black theology may yet pave the way for much indigenous theological reflection. Black theology is existential, but it is also political. It is a theology of survival, of meaning, of protest against injustice. It deals with the issues of life and death.

In this reconception process, the black theologian will become a modern apologist. He will seek to be true to the "givenness" of the eternal message of God's redemptive revelation and action in and through Christ. The black man in the context of the black experience will provide the "situation" in which he will pursue his task. The vital issues of the Christian faith will be reexamined and reinterpreted in terms of bondage and deliverance. The black theologian must deal with the hard questions and the problems of an oppressed people who seek liberation in the here and now rather than in the afterlife, though the one does not, indeed must not, exclude the other. The issue is one of priority. We have had "heaven"—now we want some of this earth. Thus, our reconception of the faith will seek to answer the question as to how we may be men and Christians at the same time. The mission of black theology is plain. It is the alternative to a mass exodus of blacks from the Christian faith in this time of black consciousness, power, and liberation. If a radical

distortion of the faith were the end product of our reconception, then our effort would be wasted. The fact is,
however, that our new humanity in Christ is the essence
of the good news. We become *dignified* and *free* persons
through our saving relationship with Christ, and this has
a great deal to do with how we ought to treat one another.

Models in theological discourse have been treated
most insistently by Ian Ramsey in recent theology. But
selecting a model for theology is as old as Christian theology itself. Between the third and the fifth century of
the Christian era a Christological model was accepted.
The concept of *enhypostasia* was approved. The issue concerned whether Christ was two natures in one person,
two natures and two persons (divine and human), or one
person in which the human nature was merged into the
divine nature. According to the orthodox view, Christ was
one person and two natures, truly divine and truly human.
The model of the hypostatic union won out in the Christological controversies and ever since has been a kind of
ecumenical theological consensus.

In our time there are ways of using this model as we
draw upon our imagination. The church may be seen as an
extension of the incarnation. The Bible may be viewed as
witnessing to Christ. The Christocentric model, as interpreted in Barth, becomes a way of working this model.
Other theological models are existential, process, evolu-
tionary, and hope.

Black theology will need to give priority to the experiential foundations of faith. A method that is psychosocial
and cultural will be more appropriate than a metaphysical
model. The descriptive-confessional method is closer to
what we need. We are describing our response to the Chris-

tian faith in the context of the black experience. In some sense we are allowing a manifestation of our experience of the "holy" to provide the symbols or the images that are to receive theological treatment. We do not desire to force prepackaged theological categories upon our experience. We seek an increasing acquaintance with the faith of our fathers in Africa and the New World as a matrix out of which a theological treatment of the Christian faith may take shape.

Johannes Pedersen has indicated how theological concepts may emerge from the culture of a people.[14] He describes the history and culture of the Israelites, their family life, community life, and cult practice. Against this background, he seeks an understanding of their theology. From Pedersen's study we learn two fundamentals: first, there is a direct relation between culture and theology; second, it is possible that the most meaningful symbols and images come forth from the history and culture of a people.

African peoples are not people of a Book. There is a strong reliance upon the spoken word and the continuity of kinship ties as a means of transmitting a religious tradition. The spontaneous sermon, the apprenticeship training of younger ministers by older ones, and a strong oral tradition illustrate how this heritage is reflected in the black church. A people of oral traditions is more dependent upon a culture-based approach to theology than is a people of a Book. We should assume, therefore, that what Pedersen has recorded about the relation between culture and theology in Israel will be equally evident among Africans and Afro-Americans.

A symbol is a type of image drawn from the world of space and time to point to a transcendent reality. It may be a cross, stained-glass windows, liturgy, concepts, and a number of other things that make up the paraphernalia of religion. A symbol is a space-time phenomenon that points to supernatural reality. There is a relationship between a symbol and that to which it points. This distinguishes a symbol from a sign. A sign is merely a pointer. It tells us where we are going but not what to expect when we arrive at our destination. A sign is objective in relation to what it signifies. A symbol, on the other hand, participates in that which it expresses at the same time that it points beyond itself to a transcendent reality. In knowing a symbol, we are led to an understanding of the internal nature of that which it indicates. In the language of John Baillie's "mediated immediacy," the symbol as a medium becomes transparent to that which is mediated. Tillich's familiar observation that in Jesus as the Christ existence becomes completely transparent to essence is a superb conceptual way of stating the matter.[15]

A symbol is unique and personal, but it may express the universal as well. The interpretative role of symbol is apparent as we develop an ethnic perspective in theology— one that moves from the experiences of a particular oppressed people to all oppressed people. The role of a symbol is to reveal a reality. A symbol is only a means, and when it becomes an end, we lapse into idolatry. A symbol is to serve the God we worship. One important symbol in black theology is the "humanity of Christ." The Son of Man who suffers with the disinherited becomes a fitting symbol of "the human face of God." Through this symbolism the oppressed have the assurance that we have a benevolent Creator and Provider.

Everett M. Stowe provides a basic statement on symbols as they are defined and used.

What is of great importance for man as the *animal symbolicum* is the process of constructive activity within man as he encounters and molds these symbolic forms. Man's response to existence is active or constructive and not merely passive. He translates his experience through symbolic transformation. The brain in its symbolic transformation of experiential data is a fountain of spontaneous ideas. The sensuous and the intelligible flow together and the image and the meaning merge in the symbol. The human understanding and the spirit are "image-needing" and symbolically disclose what is beyond them.[16]

Ladislas Segy shows how the contemporary African artist may share the collective beliefs of his people in magico-religious animism. He gives tangible expression to those deep-seated traditional beliefs as he provides body and shape for them. Image-making is a process by which external form is given to an inner vision.[17] This is close to what "image-thinking" in black theology must do.

It is to be expected that symbols for black theology will emerge not only out of Scripture and the Christian tradition but also out of African and Afro-American experience. We shall be open to this latter body of experience, but we must not create idols out of these symbols. We must not allow these images to crowd out the vision of Him who alone is the life, light, and truth of God. As the Zen masters put it, we need a finger to point to the moon, but we must not confuse the pointing finger with the moon. Though the reference here is to what we have called a sign, we must remember that symbols also are designed to mediate the immediacy of God. When God is truly present, it would be spiritual poverty to confuse the medium with the supreme reality.

Since black religious experience is mainly an oral tradition and since it is more intuitive than conceptual, we need a way of doing theology that is based primarily upon image-thinking.[18] Imagination is writ large in black experience. This makes religion a cohesive aspect of black culture. The arts, poetry, music, and the like, are closely associated with religion. Symbols emerging out of various forms of black expression can inform theology, since all theology is reflection upon religious experience.

2

Ethnicity and Theology

Black theology will need to give full expression to the particularity of the black religious experience while not neglecting the universal character of religion. The movement will be from the particular to the universal. This means that some attention should be given to the relationship between ethnicity and theology in the black experience of religion.

I agree with Martin E. Marty that "peoplehood" should be limited to those groups which have a claim on some sort of common ethnic origin and orientation.[1] This means, for example, that white women and men belong to the same ethnic group, while black Americans and American Indians do not. The so-called universal theology in America has actually been "white theology." Black theologians such as James Cone are correct in accentuating the particularity of the black experience as a proper context for theological construction.[2] Furthermore, the distinction between "white ethnics" and blacks is very important. The competition between the white immigrants and the blacks for housing and jobs accounts for much bloodshed in urban America.

Ethnicity is distinct from the "one world" ideological thesis projected by some liberals in the name of "the brotherhood of man." Ethnicity was viewed by these liberals as outmoded, for it was seen to represent a sense of a special ancestral identification with some portion of mankind. But *ethnicity* should not be locked into the mind-set of those who identify it with the absence of literacy and a relative isolation from civilized life. It is not tradition-directed, nor is it tied to the type of folk-history perspective that exalts the primitiveness of group life.[3] *Peoplehood* expresses the sense of ethnicity implied here. *Ethnicity* is derived from the Greek *ethnos* meaning "people" or "nation." We are concerned with a group with a shared feeling of peoplehood as an "ethnic group." [4]

Recently, as I registered for the annual convention of a group made up primarily of middle-aged, affluent white Americans, I was deeply disturbed by remarks made in my presence. An elderly white woman from Dallas, Texas, was telling her friends about her experiences at the Library of Congress. We were in the same line. She had been very polite to me, assuming that my presence was quite proper and respectable. She repeatedly said that there were only blacks to wait on her at the Library of Congress and that they were not able to find anything. She wanted to know what us white, intelligent people were going to do if after traveling halfway across the country we were not able to get to information in the Library of Congress because ignorant blacks had taken over. She either considered me a chocolate-coated white man, or she was unaware of the sense of ethnic identity that has accompanied the new black consciousness. My sense of peoplehood meant that every word was a personal insult to me. She may as well have been speaking in the presence of the blacks at the Library of Congress. I am certain, however, that in their presence she would have gotten a dose of her own medicine.

Gayraud S. Wilmore's essay "Ethnic Identities and Christian Theology" is highly suggestive for our intention here.[5] Wilmore indicates that we must speak of black Americans as an ethnic group along with Jews, Puerto Ricans, Polish immigrants, and others. He points out that in America we have not correlated ethnic identity with Christian theology. The WASP identity has been taken for granted. The theology of race relations has centered around the Fatherhood of God and the brotherhood of man. God and society were seen as relating to individuals rather than to races and groups. Reform would result from individual regeneration apart from membership in self-conscious racial or cultural groups. But now we are beginning to realize that racial and cultural differences are important factors for understanding and appreciating the complexity and variety of the human family. Wilmore observes: "God has not absolutized the way of life of any one race or nation." [6] What is needed is a recognition and appreciation of ethnic differences without a corresponding evaluation from one's own group downward.

A common ancestry is shared by black Africans, especially West Africans, and Afro-Americans.[7] This has been tampered with by various forms of colonialism. Colonialism is here defined broadly as various types of human oppression. In black America as in black Africa, colonialism has been experienced in terms of the victimization of

blacks and Africans by white oppressors. This does not
overlook the fact of the inner exploitation of Africans and
blacks by Africans. The fact is that white oppression intensifies the internal exploitation of the oppressed. The role
of the Western white man in the history of the modern
world as the archoppressor of colored peoples is morally
inexcusable.

There is continuity as well as discontinuity between the
African past of black Americans and their present situation. Black American culture is synthetic. We have to deal
with a cultural doubleness. We do not remember our past
and until rather recently many black Americans had no
desire to remember their African antecedents. They were
ashamed of the "dark continent." They had formed their
own estimate of their worth according to the image of
black in the white mind. A preconscious contempt for
Africa and a resulting self-hatred were widespread.

Benjamin Mays has spoken almost incessantly against
the high rate of homicides among blacks. He puts it em-
phatically when he speaks of blacks saying that they hate
Whitey, but at the same time it is "Blackie" killing
"Blackie." We must all join Mays in this concern and do
all we can to denounce and alleviate this human tragedy.
But we must deal with the cause and not merely with the
symptom. Why do blacks hate and kill each other in
such large numbers? Does self-hatred have anything to do
with it? Is this self-hatred a result of the impact of the
white man's declaration of black inferiority? While Mays
does not see any relationship between this tragedy and
black theology, my view is that this is close to the heart
of black theology.

Black theology must see blacks killing blacks not merely

as a cultural fact but as a theological problem to which the black church must address itself. Black theology is to contribute to a new self-image which would enable blacks to affirm their inherent worth independent of the estimate of black life among many whites. "Black is beautiful" means more than an Afro hair style and African attire. It has a profound theological meaning. Black life is of supreme worth. This worthfulness of black life is God-given and not man-bestowed. In addition to self-contempt we must deal with bad socioeconomic conditions, substandard education, insecure family life, and all the ills of the black poor. This has a lot to do with what whites have done and are doing to blacks. Many psychological problems among blacks have sociological causes deeply rooted in white racism.

A few months ago I preached to inmates in a federal penitentiary in a dark ghetto in a Northern city. The prison population was largely young and black. The prison was set in the black community. In locating the prison, I stopped at a local gas station. The black attendant who directed me to the prison said that he had been an inmate when he was young. Such prisons are often the "graduate school" for boys and the "finishing school" for girls. Why, I asked myself, did the city fathers locate the penitentiary and the city jail in the center of a black neighborhood? The prison is for many black youth a symbol of adulthood. Growing up meant going to prison. Not only the prison but all the bad conditions that breed crime were present, making prison an almost self-fulfilling prophecy. As one pondered the plight of these "children of the storm," one had to admire those young people who were strong enough to remain out of prison as well as those who came to themselves while confined in prison. This is the kind of situation with which black theology and the black church must be concerned. There must be a direct relationship between belief, thought, and worship and the deliverance of these captives. Put this way, the mission of black theology in the service of the black church and community is clear and urgent. This illustration points to the manner in which appreciation for our heritage relates to the affirmation of our cultural history.

To black Americans, Africa will perhaps always be a foreign place. It is, however, the place we came from. There exist blood ties and shared genetic characteristics between Africans and blacks, as well as a common experience of oppression. There is a similar temperament, a corresponding oral tradition, and much in the musical and folkloric traditions that is similar. Religion that draws upon the total human situation reflects much in common. What we have outlined as similar in both cultures may have universal characteristics. Blacks and Africans, however, have genetic and historical-cultural roots in common. It is for this reason that blacks look to Africa rather than elsewhere for the background of their heritage. For example, a strong family system exists in China as well as in Africa. But the Chinese family system is ethicoreligious, while the African outlook is religioethical. We have some indication that the black church became a family for blacks whose family life was disrupted by the separation caused by the slave auction block. Could this indicate the deep religious roots of the social organization of African life? It makes sense for black Americans to trace their cultural roots in Africa just as the Koreans and the Japanese trace much of their cultural heritage to China.

Those who refuse to consider any evidence of the African influence upon black culture also have to bear the burden of proof.[8] Blacks who await conclusive and objective evidence lose the psychological benefits of personal worth associated with a sense of cultural continuity. All black Americans will not be as fortunate as Alex Haley, who traced his ancestry in Africa to a particular tribe. Most blacks do not need a *real* home in Africa; they need a *symbolic* home there. It is only human to seek this historic and cultural continuity. Southern Presbyterians are proud of the Scottish roots of their faith. This does not imply that there is any plan to emigrate in large numbers to Scotland. This is the type of thing we have in mind between blacks and Africa.

Our quest is complicated by the oppressions we have endured in the New World, together with the rejection of first-class citizenship associated with this experience. We are "marginal" people, neither African nor fully American; yet in some sense we are both. The failure of Americans to allow blacks to melt in the "melting pot" has made this "search for the new land" most urgent in the period of black consciousness. It is tied into the psychological as well as the social liberation of blacks. We no longer have an attitude of contempt for our African and Afro-American past. To appreciate this aspect of our heritage does not require a total rejection of the best we can derive from our exposure to the Euro-American heritage. Being Western and African, our "doubleness" is authentic. We may yet be a most important bridge to humanize relations between the West and the Third World. In a real sense, we participate deeply in both worlds at the same time.

Afro-Americans will have to face realistically what

W. E. B. Du Bois described as their "doubleness." Blacks seeking an identity with Africa through changing their names, wearing African dress, studying African history, traveling or even emigrating to Africa, will need to face this doubleness, this reality of "two souls in one dark body." Africa is not merely a land of countries; it is a land of hundreds of peoples with a variety of cultures, languages, and religions. Pan-Africanism is a marvelous concept for those seeking a continuous heritage with their African ancestry, but in fact it is a very complicated matter. We know that the division of the African continent into colonies was agreed upon by the European powers at the Berlin West Africa Conference of 1884–1885. This division was for the advantage of the exploiters; it did not honor the traditional social divisions of the Africans. The European exploiters plundered the African societies, extracting the rich natural resources for the home territories and at the same time imposing alien culture, language, and religion upon their victims. This means that upon independence, African states developed their own states along the lines imposed by the European powers. African peoples cut across national boundaries according to culture and religion. They are often divided by European languages and customs. As if this were not sufficiently confusing, much of Africa in the extreme south is still under military rule. Neocolonialism in its economic and psychological forms is widespread and so are nepotism, corruption, disease, and famine. Enough has been said to indicate the difficulty involved in a utopian concept of a mass emigration to black Africa as a panacea. It is obvious that Africa needs the best skilled and educated American blacks; but these are the ones who have a better chance at home. Blacks en masse would not be welcomed by Africans, because they would be a liability rather than an asset.

Between Africa and blacks there are not only spatial distance and cultural differences; there is a time difference as well. We have gone through a process of deculturation and acculturation that has altered our view of time and history. I gave a lecture to a conference treating the African heritage of black Americans. The meeting began an hour late. This cut into my lecture and discussion time. The conference representative who introduced me indicated that all was well since the conference was operating on "African time." When I had completed the lecture, there was a desire to have a long discussion. It happened that my two youngest children were in Bible school. Since my wife was on vacation, they were dependent upon my being there to collect them on time. It became necessary for me to remind the group that, even though the conference began according to "African time," I would have to leave momentarily in order to pick up my kids according to "American time."

The fact that we have not been accepted into the mainstream means that we have maintained a subculture as part of our quest for meaning and sanity. This subculture is what Joseph Washington calls "tribalism." The fact that this subculture has been essential to our existence accounts for the persistence of "Africanisms" in our lifestyle and especially in our religious experience and cult practice. Black religious experience is Afro-American. We are in essence a people whose religious roots are in the villages and forests of Africa. Thus, our religious heritage was not lost in slavery. We did not get our religious enthusiasm from the Great Awakening or from the great American revivalists; we already had it. A Nigerian divinity student of mine said he was more at home in the mass churches in the inner city of Washington, D.C., than he was in the church he had served as pastor back in Nigeria, which was sponsored by the Southern Baptists. The reason was that his church there was completely controlled by the sponsoring group, which rejected any input from the African religious tradition. It is therefore inadequate to treat black religion primarily from a conversionist thesis. This causes one to miss the deep religious tradition that Afro-Americans inherited from their forefathers. This faith of our black forefathers is with us still in spite of slavery, repression, and discrimination.

Social segregation alone has not kept blacks from fulfillment in the white church. Our "African temperament" in religion as well as culture has done this. It is necessary to trace our religious heritage back to precolonial Africa in order to understand fully our peoplehood and our religion. As one who has studied extensively the religions of man, from written sources and on the field in Asia and Africa, I have found Africa as rich in spiritual resources as any place, including India. We cannot go wrong in the quest for the roots of religious experience in such a variegated forest of religious expression as Africa provides. It was a cultural and religious shock for me to go from the heart of Africa to so-called "advanced" countries of Western Europe and to observe the paganism and spiritual barrenness so prevalent in those latter countries. We did not come to America as a culturally naked or a spiritually barren people.

We are American as well as African. More than three

hundred years is a long time. We could not possibly co-exist in a pluralistic society for such a long time without having our character and world view greatly transformed by association. Unlike the American Indian, we were not killed en masse or driven to the reservation. We were enslaved. We became the involuntary servants of the white man. We were in the fields and in the big house. This meant that we were closely associated with whites and absorbed much of their culture. White males took black women as lovers and begot children by them. Black mammies became the real mothers of many white children. Even today black women mother white children while neglecting their own out of economic necessity. In many cases black mothers bear and feed their own children and give their love to white children. Being close to whites, we aspired to the cultural, educational, and spiritual values of this society. Even those who could not realize those values for themselves lived through their children, who frequently realized some of those things unrealized by their forefathers. Passing through this process we have become Americans in the sense that our outlook is patterned after the society in which we live. It is factual to conclude that American blacks are Afro-American. On one hand, we are bearers of an ancient culture from Africa, and on the other hand we are those who participate in the value system of a Euro-American society into which we have not been fully accepted. This is our fate and our destiny.

Black religion is the stuff out of which black theology is forged. George B. Thomas put the matter this way:

> It is black religion which speaks deeply to the inner life of reality in the black experience as expressive reality. . . . Black religion binds people in a qualitative human life style

approximating the intentional will of God. . . . Black people have understood in the deepest and tenderest terms
the undergirding security which comes from trusting in a
God who cares, binds, comforts and consoles His children. . . . Black religion is for black people a covenantal
experience of feeling, knowing and believing God.[9]

A black political theology will seek a balance between
the quest for meaning and protest against injustices. A life
must be purposeful if it is to rise above the level of mere
existence—or a type of living death. But it must also be
prepared to oppose dehumanization and all threats to authentic existence if it is to be worth living.

The religious experience of black folk has provided
both these assets. The Christian faith as appropriated and
understood has enabled us to survive though " 'buked and
scorned." Our life through faith has been filled with meaning. We have had an inner logic to our existence in spite
of all adverse circumstances. Instead of giving up and con-
cluding that life is empty, we have clung to a hard core of
purpose that has brought us through. Faith in the God who
made himself known in Christ has made the difference in
our lives.

Blacks have developed through their faith and experience an almost superhuman indifference to pain. It is as if
the long night of suffering has steeled blacks against the
tragic odds that are operating against tomorrow. An Army
chaplain, himself a black man of rank and distinction, having been decorated for his courage, indicated that he had
more difficulty preparing his white soldiers for possible
death than he did his black soldiers. He did not know how
to account for this. We are suggesting that our incessant experience of suffering has enabled us to transmute this

suffering into a purpose-filled life. We are a people who survived the Middle Passage, slavery, and constant discrimination and who still shout in church and possess "the gift of laughter." By somehow maintaining sanity in an inhuman, racist situation, we have overcome—apparently not in spite of, but because of, what has happened to us. As black psychiatrists W. H. Grier and P. M. Cobbs put it, blacks have taken what was intended to be a noose and made out of it a receptacle of moral power.[10] While Cobbs and Grier repudiate black religion in favor of a black ethic, it is my position that black religion is the source and sustainer of black ethics.

It is disturbing to see the young repudiate the faith that sustained their black forefathers and made life possible for them. The youths have only experienced the minor blows resulting from racism, whereas their black forefathers marched by faith through the very flames of hell and into the present, undaunted and unafraid. A religious experience that has brought such fulfillment, comfort, and strength for our people is surely worth having and should not be glibly discounted as a mere opiate. It should not be abandoned without thoughtful examination. Yet almost daily we see black youth snap their fingers in derision against one of the richest spiritual traditions known to man. A people cannot make it without meaning, especially if they are an oppressed people seeking liberation. The mission of black theology is to interpret this experience in order that young and old may be able to appreciate the deep religious roots of black culture. It is important that those who study black history and the black arts should also study the history of the black church and the meaning of black religion. This study will indicate that our suffering has not bred that bitterness and despair which is more deadly to the self than it is to those who have caused the suffering. What we need is meaning and hope if we are to make the proper protest against injustice to experience the liberation we seek.

We would be remiss to deal with meaning in black religious experience and omit protest as important to the black religious experience. Both meaning and protest are important if we are to be free. The quest for meaning is important in overcoming the personal identity crisis. Protest against injustices is related to our quest for peoplehood. We cannot be liberated as individuals unless we are a free people, and we cannot be liberated as a people unless we know personal freedom.

Black spirituals speak of life and death, as Howard Thurman writes. They are also social protest songs, as Miles Mark Fisher has pointed out. Recently James Cone addressed himself to the spirituals as liberation documents for blacks. Cone puts it this way:

> The spirituals are historical songs which speak about the rupture of black lives; they tell us about a people in the land of bondage, and what they did to hold themselves together and to fight back.[11]

As early as 1939 John Lovell, Jr., professor of English at Howard University, wrote concerning the protest message in black spirituals. He lists components of what he designates "the true social interpretation" of the spirituals as follows:

> First, there is the Negro's obsession for freedom, abundantly proved by every first hand document connected with the slave himself. . . . Second was the slave's desire for

justice in the judgment upon his betrayers which some might call revenge. And third was his tactic of battle, the strategy by which he expected to gain an eminent future. These three are the *leitmotif* of nearly every spiritual.[12]

William C. Stuttles, Jr., asserts that the ideological cause of rebellion was often rooted in the slave's radical religion. It was the radical religious perspective of the slave that provided "the stylization, the sort of insistency that led to revolutionary protests" in New World slave societies. He observes:

> No single formula is likely to explain all the possible connections between the slave's radical, religious bent and his radical, political ones. Yet, at least one significant generalization can be made concerning religion and purposeful violence among the slaves: in combination, they represented the slave's most creative response to the contradictions and tensions within new world slave societies.[13]

The "double meaning" of black religion as set forth by Vincent Harding in his fine essay is very instructive.[14] But it is my view that the meaning and survival characteristics of black religion are just as native and important as the protest and rebellion dimensions. Furthermore, among those who have resisted oppression, there have been prophets of hate and prophets of love. The intensity of motivation from religion has been great for both. Nat Turner illustrates the former position and Martin Luther King, Jr., the latter. What we observe, then, is "a variety of religious experience" in black religion and more than one means of protest against injustice.

Like all vital religion, black religion is both priestly and prophetic. As wholesome religion contains succor and demand, comfort and protest, even so it brings the religious and the political dimensions of life together. Radical religions provide a transcendent frame of reference and judgment to bear upon the social and political situation. The universal is expressed through the particular. Black religion in its best expression brings man's whole life together. Blacks have not been afforded the luxury of juxtaposing full hearts and empty stomachs. We are an oppressed people and are forever shocked by the scandal of particularity. Suffering is concrete and personal for all black people and to an excessive degree for the black poor. Black religious nationalism, underpinned by a consciousness of the unity of the history and the experience of all black people, has created a fellow feeling in the black community. We now know, as our African forefathers did, that "because I am, we are." We know that we will never be free as individuals until our people are free. Black religious radicalism has sponsored and continues to sponsor acts of liberation from white oppression. The very nature of the black presence in this society indicates a constant protest against injustice. Our religion is one of *resistance,* and we know well from history and experience that he who would be free must strike the first blow. Protest against racism is inherent in the black religious experience. It is out of this context that black theology must forge its creed.

Much of our energy as a people has been expended on survival in a hostile social environment. This is why so much black religion has been compensatory. When black folk tales relate how the rabbit outsmarted the fox, a reality of black life is being described—that of weakness overcoming strength.[15] We are a people who have had to carve out a destiny in an environment in which the cards have been stacked against our very survival. We have not been expected to make it. And yet we have survived to make it, because we were so determined. In the movie *Sounder,* the oldest son describes to his schoolmates the hardships of his life. A fellow schoolmate recounts how he saved his sister from drowning even though he couldn't swim. No one believed his story except a boy who had known great hardships. When the teacher asked him to explain his reasoning, he related how his mother and her children raised a crop while the father served time for stealing to feed his hungry family. Raising the crop was a matter of survival for the family. If they had not raised the crop, they would have been homeless and unemployed, for they were sharecroppers. He said, "We couldn't, but we had to!" This is the story of black life in racist America.

Whether we are considering blacks during slavery, during the lynch period, or in the urban ghettos, we are faced with a situation of such violence and indignity to the person of blacks that only the strong survive. It is of interest to keep this before good, law-abiding Christians, black as well as white, who are apt to indulge in self-congratulation concerning how they made it, or smugly to repeat the self-righteous creed, "Lord, I thank thee that I am not as other men are!"

When a people must reach up to touch bottom, when gifted children, like flowers in the wild, are "born to blush unseen, and waste their sweetness on the desert air," when those with great potential in black skin see only the ceiling and do not know of the boundless dimensions of the sky, it is not enough to dwell on the shortcomings of a people. Human nature is much the same the world over. When social and economic conditions are extremely bad, most people will just give up. At best they will seek survival at its lowest level. Fatalism and resignation settle in. But as Benjamin Mays states it, some blacks are born to rebel. When this rebellion against white oppression is motivated by strong religious conviction, a great black leader is born. This is the stuff out of which black theology emerges. Without our strong religious experience, we would long since have been crushed by the circumstances of black suffering under the heels of white oppression. We have had to deal with the ultimate issues of life and death. Ours has been a faith for survival.

Ours has been a hope against hope. Indeed, for us faith has been the substance of things hoped for. It has been based upon unseen evidence. We have overcome when there were no grounds for hope. The black faithful know what it means to reach out into the darkness and grasp the hand of God, to take a step at a time in the shadows and to find such trust better than light, better than a well-trodden path.

When I observe the close kinship ties of black families and how the young are unofficially "adopted" by the black poor, how brothers and sisters form a chain approach to education, each one helping one, then I understand the meaning of hope against hope. Those who have for a lifetime experienced a living death stir among the ashes of impossible and shattered dreams and create a living hope in their offspring. Having observed this and participated in the experience out of which I write, I am encouraged that this is the heritage of faith that, as a theologian, I am now called upon to interpret to the black faithful and to all who desire to appreciate this great legacy of the human spirit. Ours is a hope against hope, but it is a living hope. Charles L. Helton writes:

> Black people have been conditioned to a kind of tragic sensitivity which has positive dimensions. It is a sense of tragedy transformed. While having what might be called a "tragic sense of life," Black people also have a "trans-tragic hope," with a strong Biblical context. There is a unique strength within the heart of our blackness; and that strength is transformed into a gift. It is a gift in the strange sense that one is allowed to be captured by and entrapped in an institution of racism and oppression and still maintain his sanity and the perspective of faith. . . . The discovery of the power to get at and transform the depths of suffering and bondage and oppression toward hope and fulfillment and joy represents what I consider a tremendous insight into the meaning of the human experience.[16]

Christian social ethics have suffered because love has often been understood as emotional and not as also ontological and ethical as well. Justice has been separated from love, and power has been rejected as primarily evil. In a society guilty of the white declaration of black inferiority, all have not been considered free and equal. The white-dominated society has considered blacks inherently unworthy of dignified treatment as humans. Justice, which means rendering to one his due, has not been administered to the black poor. Such a result is inevitable when justice is separated from love in its ethical dimension. There has likewise been a lack of emphasis upon the sharing of power with minorities as part of the ethical context of the Christian faith. An ethic of "handouts" that insults and weakens the victim and creates false pride in the "do-gooder" is no substitute for the empowerment of the black poor. According to the understanding of faith and ethics from the side of the oppressed, love, justice, and power belong together. In the very nature of the gospel, love, justice, and power are inseparable.

Love is more than emotion. If it were only emotion, it could not be demanded or commanded. The two foci of Christian ethics proclaimed by our Lord are: love of God and love of neighbor *as one's self*. It is because we love self that we can express love on a high moral level toward others. By self-love is not meant selfishness, but self-respect. Self-hatred is one of the worst marks of oppression that racism has etched upon the black psyche. Racism has also created a false sense of worth among whites, based upon skin color. The poorest, meanest, and most illiterate white man assumes that by virtue of his white skin he is better than any black man regardless of his status. This self-glory causes many whites to measure their worth by the complexion of their skin rather than the content of their character. Thus, the black oppressed and the white oppressed both need to be liberated from a false self-image in order properly to love themselves. Racism has produced in whites a superiority complex and in blacks an inferiority complex. Both are types of enslavement of the real self. A pathology of the self follows in the path of racism. Unless we are able to overcome these false images of the self, we, as Americans, may never know the true liberty of sons of God.

Love of neighbor is also required. We are to love our neighbor as our self. The assumption is that we have a worthy attitude toward the self. Neither the white man who thinks more highly of himself than he ought to think nor the black man who thinks less highly of himself than he ought to think is prepared for love of neighbor. Christians are to be reminded that all bear the image God bestowed upon us in creation, and that even though this image has been marred by sin, it remains most precious in God's sight. We also know how dearly God has prized our worth, as demonstrated in the death and resurrection of Christ for us men and our salvation. Therefore we are to express a love for others, who through God's creative and gracious redemptive purposes share the same personal worth we have in God's sight.

This is where racism, with its emphasis upon self-glory, has distorted the Christian ethic for many white people. All men are seen as created in the image of God, yet there is always an additional "but." As Christians we must truly express love to our neighbor or we cannot truly love God. Love for God is expressed through love of neighbor. It is through love of God's image in the self and the neighbor that we manifest our love for God. There is no love of God that does not find expression among men. This expression is not love of universal man. It is love of, or for, particular men. Love of universal man is abstract. Love for particular men is concrete and personal. One can love *everybody* and not love *anybody*. But if we love somebody, we may expand that love to include many. In order to overcome racism, love must be expressed in concrete terms. This expression of love is more than emotion and sentiment. Too much love of whites for blacks has been a kind of pity that is closer to contempt than to compassion. It has too often been paternalistic and has been dispensed as if by a parent to a child. A seventy-year-old grandfather with distinction as a father, citizen, professional, and churchman was addressed by a devout white "Christian" in my presence as "boy." An expression of love that does not grant the black man his manhood is not genuine. This is why love must be associated with justice.

Justice, in its classical meaning, is rendering to one his due. The Biblical meaning of justice includes an expression of righteousness. Justice is rooted in the moral integrity of the character of God. In God's nature, justice and mercy greet each other. God is loving, but he is also just. Thus, we are to "do justly, and to love mercy." Justice is that which supports the moral character of God. Love in the Christian sense is always related to just and equal treatment of humans. Justice is always tempered by a loving concern for the God-given worthfulness of the human person. All persons bear the same image and are saved by the same grace. Just as, in the state, whites seek "law and order" without justice, even so, in the church, they seek love without justice. Love requires compassion (active love), but justice requires that the institutions of society be altered so as to make the expression of love possible. Under the conditions of sin, love can be implemented only by the "pushing" of justice. To make life more human for the oppressed and to reclaim the humanity of the oppressed as well, the racism that is built into our most cherished institutions, including our churches, must be attacked and removed "root and branch." Without this there can be "whiteanity," but there can be no genuine Christianity. God is lovingly just. Love and justice belong together and we cannot love unjustly, nor may we unjustly love.

One important reason why the black poor are pitied rather than loved and treated justly is that they are helpless and powerless people. Their state is the result of the whole history of racism and oppression in this society. It is a result of what America has done to blacks. Power is a theological as well as an ethical matter. It is essential to remember that the Christian's God is said to be all-powerful. Afro-Americans have a legacy of "power" in their behalf in God, and it spans thousands of years. The gods of the African forests are power-laden divinities who pass on power to men through various spirits. The God of the Bible, who by a mighty hand delivered the enslaved Israelites from Egyptian bondage, illustrates the attribute of power in God. God uses his power to liberate his people. God possesses absolute goodness, but he has ample power to sustain his goodness and to establish righteousness in the earth. It is this divine power which has sustained black life and nourished black hope through the long night of suffering.

It is a crucial consideration that love and justice be linked with power in black theology. Blacks have too often sought their status as humans merely from a position of weakness. We have used all types of methods to procure our rights. No one needed to take us seriously, because we spoke and acted out of a condition of powerlessness. We were despised, rejected, and brutally treated by white oppressors. The spiritual captures the experience perfectly: "I've been 'buked and I've been scorned; I've been talked about sure as you born." As a result of a new black consciousness, we have decided henceforth to bargain from a position of strength rather than weakness. Power in itself is morally neutral; it can take on the moral and theological purpose for which it is used. Black theologians and churchmen must use all the power at their disposal to liberate and humanize life for black people. The black church is a slumbering giant. A black political theology is

designed to awaken this most powerful black institution in
the cause of the liberation of the whole man.

Just as theologians of liberation in Latin America have
seized upon the term "conscientization" to describe the
liberating and humanizing aspirations of the masses of
the oppressed in Latin America, black theologians have
grafted their message onto the concept of "black power."
Black power symbolizes a number of images and ideas
drawn from black history and the black experience: black
consciousness, pride, self-respect, community control, rep-
arations, empowerment, personhood, and peoplehood.
These are some of the meanings that flood the black mind
and psyche when the words "black power" are used.

James Cone views the relation of black theology and
black power in this way:

> Black power and black theology work on two separate
> but similar fronts. Both believe that Blackness is the pri-
> mary datum of human experience which must be reckoned
> with, for it is the *reason* for our oppression and the only
> *tool* for our liberation. Black power investigates the mean-
> ing of Blackness from the political, economic and social
> condition of Black people, explicating what freedom and
> self-determination mean for the wretched of the earth.
> Black theology places the Black Power concept in its proper
> theological context, analyzing Black liberation in the light
> of the gospel of Jesus Christ. Black Theology is the theo-
> logical arm of Black Power and Black Power is the political
> arm of Black Theology.[17]

Black power points to a new mind-set, a new way of
seeing life and relations between persons. It rejects the
hero approach to black history with its tokens and super-
blacks. It requires a decolonization of the mind. It requires

that we see ourselves as equals in a society of humans, thus shattering the superiority-inferiority syndrome of whites over blacks. We say good-by to Uncle Tom; for there are no more white parents and black children. A man is a man is a man. In this new consciousness, we have come of age and will be respected and treated as men. We will no longer determine or measure our worth by our association with whites. We have a worth and an integrity in our own right that are God-given and not man-bestowed. This and more is the meaning of the new black awareness that the symbol of "black power" communicates.

White racism is a human tragedy deeply entrenched in the preconscious realm of the collective unconscious of white America. It is part of our "immoral society" which even "moral man" will need to face frankly if it is to be uprooted. Racism is a social sin and it cannot be conquered by personal evangelism alone. I was recently buttonholed by a white couple of middle years at an international convention. They were evangelicals obsessed with saving souls. They had a son in the ministry who was like-minded. When they found out that I was a minister and theologian, they immediately invited me to come out to their home state in the Midwest to speak on evangelism. It was a most difficult task for me to express gracefully my lack of enthusiasm for their version of Christianity and express my regrets for having to turn down the invitation. They were obviously puzzled and troubled by my reply. They really thought I would be interested and indeed thought they were doing me a favor. This mind-set illustrates the fact that for many the gospel has no social consciousness and is not a power for change. Black power, on the other hand, is the basis for a gospel of power for the liberation of the oppressed. The black church and the theology of the black religious experience remain evangelical, but are avowedly political. Thus, being informed by the meaning of black power, black theology has as its task the interpretation of the faith of our black fathers, which is living still.

It is proper that we should develop a theology that receives its images and meaning from our life-and-death struggle for authentic existence. This society has sought to crush blacks beneath the heels of the powerful who have marched over the humanity of our masses. The image of the black man in the white mind has been that of a nobody. There is evidence that many whites continue to think and act upon the assumption that blacks are not human. Black power not only affirms the new self-understanding that asserts our humanity; it goes on to suggest that blacks as a people must unite and take the appropriate steps to win their liberation from white oppression.

Black power, correctly understood, is freedom for responsibility in the interest of a permanent state of liberation. Self-help, self-determination, community control—all imply awesome responsibility if the experience of black liberation is to be obtained and sustained. We must, therefore, move beyond the rapping to a state of mapping. Moltmann speaks of a theology of "hope and planning." Black theology must be no less. This is where the programs in black theology and the witness of the black church must now be on the cutting edge of events. Ours must be a witness in the world. Black theology must be specific in talking about meaning and the delivery of goods and services to the black poor. What black power means is that our motto must be: "Resistance! resistance! resistance!" We view racism not merely as a social evil, but as a theological sin. We are an oppressed people who are determined to be free—to share in all the freedoms and responsibilities of our country. Liberation is not merely a secular task; it is a sacred duty as well, for life is whole. Black theology and the black church must become strong allies in the cause of black liberation.

3

The Wholeness of Man

And the LORD God formed man of the dust of the ground, and breathed into his nostrils the breath of life; and man became a living soul.[1]

The heart of the Biblical understanding of man is centered around the "image" of God in man. This is crucial for any adequate Christian theological account of man. James Weldon Johnson in his poetic sermon "The Creation" has indicated how the old-time black preacher relied upon the Bible account of creation as he discussed the origin of man. The God-given dignity of man is included in this assertion and so is his infinite worth.[2] H. Shelton Smith has indicated how the white man's understanding of man has been marred by racism. The title of his book is self-explanatory: *In His Image, But . . .*[3] According to Smith, Southern religion from 1780 to 1910 was notorious for distorting the Biblical understanding of man in order to support slavery and racism. An understanding of man in black theology will help to correct this distortion.

The African view of man is a part of the understanding

of the unity of the tribe. As we have said, emphasis is upon collective man summed up in the formula: "Because I am, we are." There is also a unity of all life. Man is vitally related to nature, God, ancestors, and the like. He enters into the whole of being, without dividing life up into parts. The African is fully conscious of the wholeness and cohesiveness of the whole of creation, within which interaction is the only way to exist.[4] The importance of man in African thought and belief is stated by John Mbiti as follows:

> African ontology is basically anthropocentric: man is at the very centre of existence, and African peoples see everything else in its relation to this central position of man.[5]

We have seen that the understanding of man in African traditional thought places great stress upon the wholeness of man and the unity of life. We have also observed that considerable emphasis is placed upon social man or man as a member of a family or tribe. The wholeness of man is found in a healthy view of personhood and peoplehood. These are the points at which racism has precipitated a crisis for the black man. Black theology must address itself to the meaning of persons in both the personal and social dimensions. The discussion here supplements my discussion in my previous volume on black theology. In that study I sought to develop a kind of outline for various doctrines. I still believe that the emphasis on human dignity there is fundamental. Here it seems best, however, to examine the relation between human liberation and a holistic view of man.

Christians have always talked about the freedom of the Christian man. Even during slavery, when blacks were still in chains, Paul's exhortation: "Slaves, obey your masters" (Col. 3:22) became a favorite text for slavery preachers and theologians. Paul could sincerely request that Philemon receive his slave Onesimus ("useful," "beneficial") as a slave in the flesh, but as a brother in the Lord (Philemon 16). The position of Paul on master-slave relations became the standard proclaimed by slavery Christianity in reference to blacks. Paul has not been fully appreciated by several black religious thinkers. Howard Thurman and Albert Cleage agree on this one point. Paul is viewed by them as a *status quo* religionist with a lack of social consciousness. Paul was indeed a conservative. In some other matters Paul is quite helpful, but he does not touch base for the oppressed at this point.

We are aware that white Christians first had to decide whether blacks had souls. Apparently they were led to believe that American Indians had souls before they believed that blacks had souls. They had to deal with a legal question that had a socioeconomic base, the question as to whether salvation and freedom from slavery are related. This was settled in a negative statement by a Virginia court: conversion and emancipation do not take place at the same time. Only theological endorsement remained necessary to make this position acceptable to church and state. In law, custom, and theology, we have the position established that the black man is only partly human. Paul became the theologian par excellence in forging an acceptable Bible-based theological stance whereby a slave can be free in the Lord and remain shackled in the chains of physical bondage. It is the position of black theology that liberation from bondage includes the whole man.[6]

The Mormon doctrine of man is inherently racist. According to Mormon doctrine, the black man is inherently inferior and the white man is inherently superior. People of dark skin made a wrong choice in the spirit world—in the preexistence affirmed by Mormon theology. Whites, the chosen people, followed Jesus. Blacks turned away from Christ and so must suffer. Blacks, being the progeny of Ham, were already cursed. But they were further cursed by God because they rejected Christ. They are not worthy of the priesthood, whereas white males are admitted to the priesthood and will reach the highest level in the Mormon "split-level" heaven.

People of dark skin, at least American Indians, may someday become "white and delightsome." At that time they may reach the highest level of celestial bliss. In the meantime, blacks are not to be admitted to the priesthood. The Church of Jesus Christ of Latter-day Saints, organized by Joseph Smith, admits blacks to its membership but not to its priesthood. This policy is based upon a document known as the Book of Abraham. It was translated by Smith from the hieroglyphics on an Egyptian papyrus scroll which came into his hands years after The Book of Mormon was published. Interpreting black skin as a mark of disfavor, that passage is the main basis for denying the priesthood to blacks. Legend and a lay ministry have codified this misconception into a dogma. Under the pressure of a militant minority of blacks, Mormons await a new revelation. Meanwhile blacks who accept the presuppositions of the Mormon creed should hope to become "white and delightsome." [7]

This false interpretation of man, in Biblical and theological terms, is to be rejected for what it is—a clear attempt to theologize the black man into inferiority and theologize the white man into superiority. It could be ignored save for the fact that this general view is held by a wider circle of white Christians than Mormons and the problem is with us still. Belief in the racial inferiority of blacks and the racial superiority of whites is deeply embedded in the personal and social outlook of white churchgoers. This is true not only of white Anglo-Saxon Protestants, but of many Roman Catholics and Jews as well. Religious institutions of this country, as well as nonreligious masses of people, are racist. Robert T. Handy observes correctly that white church historians are reluctant to treat the history of Christianity among blacks because the past comes home in the present. Handy quotes the pointed observation of Stanley M. Elkins that "there is a painful touchiness in all aspects of the subject; the discourse contains almost too much immediacy, it makes too many connections with present problems." [8]

Martin Luther King, Jr., correctly referred to racism as a cancerous growth eating away at the very fiber of American society. Not only blacks, but whites as well, are in need of being liberated from the desolation in human relations in this country based on skin color. Racism must be recognized for what it is at its source if sanity, health, and wholeness are to be restored to this land. A white minister commented at the end of one of my lectures that he never had kept any slaves. He was reminded that this does not mean that he does not possess a slavery mentality in reference to blacks and that he would need to deal with the collective guilt of racism in its present form. Racism is insidious and preconscious as well as open and conscious. It is institutional as well as individual. The effects of racism upon its victim are serious regardless of the form it takes. It is for this reason that black theology is interested not in salves but in major surgery.

This is where I see black consciousness as providing a radical perspective for ex-colonial peoples in the Third World, especially in Africa. Many Africans need to de-colonize their minds. They are too trusting of their former exploiters. In many cases they have accepted without question the values of the colonizers. We have always been marginal to this society and, therefore, we have observed the American way of life with a critical judgment.

Gabriel Setiloane, an African theologian, writes as follows:

> The difference between Black Theology enthusiasts and the Africans is that the Americans do their theologizing in the dust and heat of political warfare; hence their militancy and impatience; whereas we can claim to work in an atmosphere of physical political freedom and comparable calm.[9]

This statement does not represent a true picture of Africa as I have known it; nor of Africa as many Africans are now experiencing it. In some sense oppression in South Africa, in Uganda and in America's South and troubled urban centers, is quite similar. The social setting is different and in some cases the oppressors are black, but the victims all need a gospel of deliverance: from racism, poverty, disease. What I hope to see is a recognition of this "common cause" in the transatlantic discussion between blacks and African theologians. On the Christian understanding of man, as on most of the doctrines of the Creed, we can share mutual riches.

The black man is what Daniel Boorstin describes as

"an indelible immigrant." [10] European peoples have transcended their immigrant status, but slavery and discrimination have locked the black man into a permanent noncitizen status. He is part of a man, and a second-class citizen. *The Washington Post* of August 14, 1973, described the alarming degree to which the American volunteer army is becoming black. The socioeconomic conditions for the black male are such that he will most likely succeed as a criminal or a soldier. It is ironic that good law-abiding, patriotic, religious white Americans will, because of racism, eventually be protected by a predominantly black army. But there need be no real worry yet. For the time being, although a disproportionate number of those enlisting are black, most officers are white.

Blacks are also "invisible," as Ralph Ellison points out:

> I am an invisible man. No, I am not a spook. . . . I am a man of substance, of flesh and bone, fiber and liquids. I might even be said to possess a mind. I am invisible, understand, simply because people refuse to see me.[11]

James Baldwin observes that in the South the black man is a ward and in the North he is a victim. He warns that the country will not change until it reexamines itself and what it really means by freedom. He observes: "It is a terrible, an inexorable, law that one cannot deny the humanity of another without diminishing one's own." [12]

These black literary figures are very penetrating in their analysis of the black human condition. In the 1890's a black preacher, J. W. E. Bowen, was very perceptive when he observed that the "manhood problem" was central for blacks.[13] He saw the denial of "manhood" as the root of most evils facing blacks, personal and social, internal and external. Implied is the fact that the social evils of racism are a hindrance to the health and wholeness of blacks.

Joel Kovel has described three "types" of racial fantasies: First the *dominative* racist, who acts out the bigoted beliefs. Examples would be a night rider in the South or a member of a mob protesting open housing in Chicago. Second is the *aversive* racist, who believes in white race superiority and is more or less aware of it, but does nothing overt about it. He may lapse into dominative racism, however, if blacks get "too close." Third is the *unconscious racist,* who does not reveal racist tendencies at all.[14] In sum according to Kovel:

> Whatever a white man experiences as bad in himself . . . whatever is forbidden and horrifying in human nature, may be designated as black and projected onto a man whose dark skin and oppressed past fit him to receive the symbol.[15]

Kovel is correct when he asserts that white racism in America is no aberration, but an ingredient of our culture, and that it cannot be fully understood apart from the rest of our culture.[16] He observes, further, that the symbols and fantasies of racism have been generated by the history of race relations and sustained by the rest of our organically related culture.[17] If Kovel is correct, and there is much evidence to support his finding, it is not too much to assert that most, if not all, whites are racists. To begin with this assumption would mean that those who are really concerned would begin the kind of self-examination that could lead to discovery of the cause and the cure of racism.

Cobbs and Grier, as black psychiatrists, analyze the experience of a black boy growing up in this country.

There are all types of impediments. Schools discourage his ambitions; training for skills is often not available to him. When he does achieve, he receives compromised praise. Society seems locked against him. He lives in a society that views his growth with hostility. A nephew of mine who is a fine athlete with rare musical talent is in an integrated senior high school. The principal and most of the teachers are white. The black teachers and principals were demoted or dismissed when the schools were integrated. The kind of encouragement and counsel I received from my early teachers is absent. He performed so well in a band concert that his white peers knew he had won a first prize in their concert, but the adults in charge gave it to a white student. He quit the band in protest, disappointed and discouraged. The coach sought then to exploit his talents on the playing field. He was to be so involved in sports as to threaten his college admission and a future in a profession. In a long conversation, I was able to help him put things in perspective. This illustrates the struggle for manhood experienced by the most fortunate and gifted of our black youth.

For the black man in this country, attaining manhood is an active process. The white man regards his manhood as an ordained right. Throughout life the black man is told to hold back, to constrict, to camouflage his normal abilities. The white anxiety over the batting average of Hank Aaron, the fear that he will set a record beyond that of Babe Ruth, is fanning the flames of racism. Cobbs and Grier recall that under slavery, the black man was psychologically emasculated and totally dependent as a human being.[18] Even today black men continue to exhibit the inhibitions and psychopathology that had its genesis in the slave experience. The American heritage of racism will not, at the present time, allow the black man his proper rights and freedom. It is obvious that the white man is not prepared to share power with the black man:

> As boys approach adulthood, masculinity becomes more and more bound up with money making. In a capitalistic society economic wealth is inextricably interwoven with manhood. [It is] closely allied with power—power to control and direct other men, power to influence the course of one's own and other lives. The more one can influence, the greater the power. The ultimate power is the freedom to understand and alter one's life. It is this power, both individually and collectively, which has been denied the black man.[19]

We are told that during slavery any black man who asserted his manhood was a threat to the slave system. He was killed.[20] This meant that the black man had little choice but to express his manhood privately, as forbidden fruit. Most black boys, we are told, are fed on a steady diet of folk heroes who have distinguished themselves by sexual feats. Black men who have been otherwise outperformed by white men boast of their sexual success with white women. But we are reminded that these folk heroes are not directing armies or wielding significant political and economic power. Their "wielding of power had been in the privacy of the boudoir." [21] Our writers observe that the black man often uses sex as a means of defense, as armament, as a dagger to be symbolically thrust into the white man. An orderly in a hospital who was an acknowledged and self-conscious failure in everything he attempted was seduced by a white nurse. When he was convinced that she really wanted him sexually, he took her to bed with a vengeance. He confessed in therapy sessions that every time he possessed the girl sexually, he was making up for having sat in the back of the bus and all other humiliations. The sexual act was a way of getting revenge for generations of slavery and degradation.[22] We don't need a psychiatrist to tell us why he needed help.

Cobbs and Grier also analyze the stereotypes of black folklore, i.e., the "bad nigger." They look at the "post-clerk syndrome." This is the passive, nonassertive, and nonaggressive type who is considered "nice" by white people. He thinks and acts as if he were white and only wants to please the "Man" in order to make it. He is a direct lineal descendant of the "house nigger" of slavery who identified so completely with his master that he had no life of his own.[23] These and many other matters illustrate the psychopathology of blacks in sociological and historical perspective. What is true of black men is just as true of black women, even though their reaction to oppression is different. Bad socioeconomic conditions often lead black males to robbery and black females to prostitution. It is unfortunate that many of the new black films are feeding the stereotypes of the superbad "nigger" in those very neighborhoods which need to be improved. Even more alarming is the inaction of the black churches concerning these and other problems.

What we have observed is that the human situation under racism is one of alienation, brokenness, pathology, and sin. A doctrine of man in black theology should begin with the human condition and aim at liberation through wholeness. Wholeness is related to a total view of man as body, mind, soul, and spirit. Theologies of the body are likely to be concerned primarily with carnal man and man's place in nature. Theologies of revolution aim primarily at collective man. The approach of black theology must be existential as well as political.

It is well that our black fathers, mainly in West Africa, did not know Plato. Africans did not know of a split in human existence between soul and body or between human life and all life. The temperament of Afro-Americans is to see life whole. Timothy L. Smith has made this interesting assessment, with which I am in basic agreement:

> Although by careless classification one might lump most twentieth-century Negro pastors in the "Fundamentalist" camp, neither their social view of the Christian future nor their grasp of scriptural ideas fits the ultra-conservative Protestant mold. Black preachers still call sinners to come to Jesus and appeal to the authority of God's word in doing so; but when they speak of housing and employment, of voting rights and health care, they do not sound like Fundamentalists at all.[24]

And even though this is basically correct, there is the absence of a conscious theological position to undergird this interest in the whole man. Some black preachers who are well trained and who are deeply involved in social causes preach only priestly sermons and sing and pray about spiritual comfort here and in the afterlife. Those members who work in the educational and social programs of the church do not worship, and many of those who do worship see religion as a means to personal peace and salvation. Evangelicalism and social gospel are present, but because the minister does not operate out of a conscious theological understanding of the black situation, he is not able to relate the black rite on Sunday with programs of black liberation during the rest of the week. He needs an understanding of man which will bring wholeness to his people. This theology will have to emerge out of the black religious experience. This is where ethnicity and theology meet.

The approach to a doctrine of man for blacks will need to take Freud and Marx quite seriously insofar as they contribute to our deeper understanding of human nature. Black theology will be more concerned about the social impact upon the individual than it will about pure spirituality and mystic experience. Where piety is most present it will be socially conscious and mystic experience will be profoundly ethical, as is the case with Howard Thurman. Black theology has been dismissed as sociology by many proper theologians who insist that only scholastic theology is genuine. In understanding man, however, we will be more concerned about the meaning of the faith for black life than we will be about the approval or disapproval of critics.

Man, for most Euro-American theologians, is Promethean man. Prometheus was the Titan in Greek legend who stole fire from heaven as a gift for man. Thus, Promethean man is man "come of age," as Dietrich Bonhoeffer phrased it. Promethean man is the man of the "God is dead" theologies and many secular theologies of our time. Promethean man is a proper designation for men who are self-sufficient and powerful enough to determine their own destiny. But, as we have seen, black men in this society are not Promethean man. We need an understanding of man which touches base with the reality of our lives.

Man is not "on his own," as Ernst Bloch would have it.[25] Cone is correct: the black man in affirming his humanity says "yes" to God. But in affirming his humanity, he also says "no" to white oppression. Cone writes:

> The image of God refers to the way in which God intends for man to live in the world. The image of God is thus more than rationality, more than what so-called neo-orthodox theologians call divine-human encounter. In a world in which men are oppressed, the image is man in rebellion against the structures of oppression. It is man involved in the liberation struggle against the forces of community.[26]

It is important to black experience that man be understood in relation to God the Giver and Redeemer of life. The black man's dignity is not dependent upon the whims and fancies of those who are his oppressors. Black men's awareness of their self-worth is not dependent upon the findings of men such as Arthur Jensen, who would base the black man's low status in society upon inheritance through the genes.[27] Neither will we base our self-understanding upon a faulty theology that traces this inferiority to either God's ordained or permissive will. We know we are "somebody." God created us as "somebody." He sustains us and redeems us as beings of supreme worth. We are not limited to man's estimate of man. J. Garfield Owens in his meditations upon the spirituals observes in them protest and assurance. He points out that even black slaves held up the faith that "We are God's children." He continues:

> The slaves, dispossessed of everything, denied the privilege of pursuing earthly goods, their labor and toil all going for the enrichment of their masters, . . . could not believe that they were beyond God's loving providence.[28]

The faith of our black forefathers gave birth to a theology of hope. They learned through the acceptance of Biblical faith how to cope with what otherwise would have been an overwhelming tragedy. White Christians in the slaveholding states told the African slaves selected stories as if they were children. They desired to make them obedient so they would be gentle and docile. They described the joys of heaven and the horrors of Milton's, if not the Bible's, hell. Listening blacks interpreted these accounts for themselves in the light of their encounters with despair and hope. Such stories as Moses and the deliverance of an enslaved people, Jonah's denunciation of the Ninevites (the rich and the powerful), of Babylonian exile, of Daniel and the Hebrew children, seemed to be allegories of promise. The baby Jesus needed tenderness and care, and his incarnation in the humiliation and weakness of human flesh joined him with the meek who would inherit the earth.[29] This indicates that black men have always forged out of their experience their understanding of human existence. The Christian faith gave the black man a sense of "somebodiness" in spite of circumstances to the contrary. When he sang, "I got shoes; you got shoes, all God's children got shoes!" he was staking his worthfulness upon the promises of God. God as benevolent creator, bountiful provider, and loving redeemer was the basis of his humanity. Black children learned from bitter experience that it is better to put trust in God than confidence in men.

Our understanding of man in the Bible enables us to affirm our personhood. We have been regarded as property. Indeed the white backlash during the long, hot summers of the 1960's indicated that property was regarded as being more valuable than black life. The notion of personality, of human beings as ends, so basic to a proper understanding of Christian anthropology, is absent from the theology of race relations for many whites.

White mobs hanged, shot, burned, gouged, flogged, drowned, impaled, dismembered, and blowtorched to death almost 550 blacks, including aged cripples, young boys, and pregnant mothers, in lynchings from 1919 to 1939. Devout Protestants were among the participants at these "modern Golgothas." These would-be servants of the Lord encouraged or silently acquiesced in lynchings. These evangelical Protestants saw no relationship between these acts of human torture and their deep piety. They were against smoking, drinking, and illicit sex. They closed down pool rooms, but they were silent on lynching.[30] Reinhold Niebuhr observed correctly: "I don't find people belonging to churches giving a guarantee of emancipated race attitude or a high type of political morality." [31]

The agonizing words of Du Bois writing from Atlanta in 1906 might well be repeated today:

> A city lay in travail, God our Lord, and from her loins sprang twin Murder and Black Hate. Red was the midnight; clang, crack and cry of death and fury filled the air and trembled underneath the stars when church spires pointed silently to Thee. And all this was to sate the greed of greedy men who hide behind the veil of vengeance! [32]

In words akin to the prophets of the Old Testament, Du Bois observes: "We are not better than our fellows, Lord, we are but weak and human men." [33] He continues:

> And yet whose is the deeper guilt? Who made these devils? . . . Who ravished and debauched their mothers and

their grandmothers? Who bought and sold their crime, and
waxed fat and rich on public iniquity?
   Thou knowest, good God! [34]

It is against this background that through faith and the
understanding of selfhood we have affirmed the dignity and
infinite value of black life under God. We need an understanding of human nature that can bring to black people,
under the conditions of their existence, sanity and wholeness. A perfectly rational interpretation of man, however
much applauded by white theologians, would be "dry
bones" for the faith of the black masses if it did not take
seriously their life- and death-struggle in this society. We
are a people who live an extreme existence on the edge
of despair. Perhaps I am not speaking to the black university professor who operates out of the gilded tower of
an Ivy League university. But the desperation of the black
poor is bad and getting worse.

The man with a black face who packs his lunch daily
and waits on the edge of the city to bargain for a day's
work with a white boss understands of what I speak. The
black mother who leaves her little ones before daybreak
to catch a bus to the suburbs to care for the children and
the homes of the rich and the powerful in order to buy
bread and pay rent, but who is too tired at eventide to feed
and love her own children, can understand our meaning.
In interpreting man in Christian theological perspective,
the black theologian has to bring a meaning of self-respect
to people who can no longer accept themselves. According
to the Christian faith, we are all God's children, and as
Creator and Redeemer of life God accepts us even though,

according to our self-estimate or the estimate of others, we are unacceptable.

Man, in black religious experience, is existential. Man is a being who has the means of self-knowledge. He has memory, understanding, and will, as Augustine noted. He is a free and dignified self. In man, freedom and responsibility are united, and he shares equally in both. He has the powers of self-transcendence and self-judgment. Man is capable of self-criticism as well as of the criticism of others. He is a being with several levels of awareness. He is preconscious, conscious, and self-conscious.

Man is great and wretched at the same time, as Pascal notes. He is a mean between nothing and all. He participates in being and nonbeing, as Tillich points out. He is a mean between two infinities. Man is capable of rising to noble heights or sinking to diabolical depths. He is "fearfully and wonderfully made," observes the psalmist, "little less than God."

In black religious experience, man is social. God made man for fellowship. "No man is an island, no man lives alone." Man cannot be fulfilled without sociability. Our freedom is limited by the boundaries of other selves. We are persons-in-community. Our wholeness as persons depends upon a healthy group life in families, communities, and nations. Our theological understanding of man is concerned about the ethics regulating interpersonal and intergroup relations. Reinhold Niebuhr and John Bennett are correct in speaking of "immoral society" and the need for social salvation. Theologians who have fled totalitarianism, men such as Tillich, refer to the gestalt of evil—the "demonic" in human society and the need for a structure of

justice to confront these "principalities and powers."
Howard Thurman observes that "man would never accept the absence of community as his destiny." [35] The term
ujamaa is used in East Africa to refer to "familyhood." [36]
Man cannot be whole without the experience of community
as fulfillment. God has created us for sociability and this
is the very essence of man as man. Social consciousness is
built into the very nature of Christian anthropology. Black
theology is concerned for the liberation of the oppressed
in the social setting where men must find authentic existence. Since racism produces an unhealthy social environment for black existence, black theology presents insights and directions as to how black men under God and
among other humans may reclaim their manhood and their
humanity.

Man in black experience is a creature. He is a physical
being in need of the goods and services for a dignified and
meaningful life. It is not the opinion of black Christians
that God expected them to be "hewers of wood and drawers of water," as some devout churchgoers in white skin
sincerely believe. According to black theology, then, we
are to be concerned about our bodily life. We believe in
the sanctity of the *sōma* ("body"). The body is worthful in
its own right because it is a part of God's creation. The
fleshly life of man was in God's creative purpose when he
declared it "good" and in his re-creative purpose when the
Word became flesh. Just as the Hebrews viewed man as a
whole, body and soul, even so our African forefathers affirmed the unity and wholeness of life. A theological view
of man emerging out of the Bible and out of our African
religious heritage would not present a division in man's
life. The influence of Plato accounts for the split image.

Furthermore, slavery Christianity advocated the continued split for blacks in order that economic gain might accrue from human bondage. The unfortunate thing is that the American theologians seem now to be victims of their own devious intentions. What better reason do blacks need for a reconception of theology truer to the gospel and more redemptive for them in the quest for liberation from oppression?

Finally, man is political in black theology. John Mbiti, in outlining the hierarchical scheme of religion in African societies, offers this description: First comes the healer, then the prophet, then the evangelist, and finally the baptizer. The tragedy of American Christianity is that we desire only to evangelize and baptize. We omit too often the healing and the prophetic imperatives of our faith.

In June of 1973, Billy Graham came to Atlanta. His chairman was Thomas Cousins, a wealthy real estate developer. The estimated cost of the crusade was a half million dollars. But what was most disturbing was how Graham described his ministry. He said:

> My objective is to get people converted to Jesus Christ so that their sins are forgiven; when they die, they'll go to Heaven. They'll spend eternity with God, and secondly to make them better citizens here on earth.[37]

He continued:

> I really want to be just a preacher. I don't want to do anything else . . . except to preach the gospel and win people for Christ. . . .[38]

The absence of blacks from the bleachers of the Atlanta Stadium may be explained by their wickedness and indifference to the gospel. It would be more adequately explained by their need to hear a gospel of healing and prophecy that is absent in a purely personal gospel.

Our understanding of the gospel is political. Man in black theology is a being who exercises power on behalf of his authentic manhood. The Christian man is not necessarily a *status quo* citizen. When the existing order is immoral and unjust, he exercises those legal and political means necessary to make the structures and institutions of society more responsive to the humanization of life. All those who are now waking up to the American dream are aware that "the powers that be" are not always ordained by God, even if Paul said so. If he had lived in the latter part of the first century, this statement would most likely not appear in his letter to the Romans. Blacks who have experienced America, often as a nightmare, have known all along that something is radically wrong with a society which remains so racist, inhuman, and unjust to the largest minority in the country because of the complexion of their skin.

4

The Pain
and Power of God

We have indicated that a theology with an ethnic consciousness will need to make use of symbolic language. We referred to image-thinking as having greater currency in black theology than concept-thinking. "Pain" and "power" as attributes of God tell us something about the nature of God and his benevolent and providential concern for the oppressed. Rubem A. Alves asserts that God is a suffering God.[1] William Jones argues that "theodicy" is to be the controlling category of black theology. Jones observes:

> Black suffering is maldistributed, enormous and non-catastrophic. Its unique quality forces us to ask: Is God a white racist? And to raise this question, in the final analysis, is to introduce the theodicy question.[2]

Jürgen Moltmann is correct in pointing out that in situations like Auschwitz, we face evil not in its naturalistic form, as in the Lisbon earthquake of 1755, but in its political form. We confront what he describes as the "crimes of history." [3] In America, racism is such a crime. Thus in treating the question of God the black theologian has to face this problem head on.

Thomas W. Ogletree attempts to employ "power" as a concept in forging a constructive statement on God. He writes:

> Language about God will be linked to concrete happenings within the social process which in incalculable ways release creative, new energy in men by which they are enabled to transcend the destructive limits of their old situation and enter into the realization of new possibilities of human fulfillment. . . . The primary category for expressing the divine reality is "creative power," a category which gains concreteness in relation to the problems of power present in social and political processes.[4]

It is significant that Ogletree arrives at this view as he observes the movements involving blacks and radical students. While many of the students of the New Left of the 1960's have abandoned their political interest and have turned to ecological and psychedelic approaches to theology, blacks still demand a strong theology for social change.

Nathan Wright, Jr., writing in the late 1960's, observed the importance of the concept of power in black theology. According to Wright, all men need the power to *become*. Without power, life cannot become what it must be. Recalling that the Greeks' word for power (*bia*) and life (*bios*) are closely associated, he concludes that power is basic to life.[5] Wright sees this fact as having important implications for a doctrine of God.

> In religious terms, a God of power, of majesty and of might, who has made man to be in His own image and likeness, must will that His creation reflect in the immediacies of life His power, His majesty and His might. Black

power raises, for the healing of humanity and for the renewal of a commitment to the creative religious purpose of growth, the far too long overlooked need for power, if life is to become what in the mind of its Creator it is destined to be.[6]

Having introduced the images of "pain" and "power" in reference to God, we may observe that what we are really after is an estimate of the "humanity of God." The question to which black Americans must address themselves is: Does God care? The occasion of the question is black suffering. We have already observed that black suffering is a moral evil rather than a natural happening. Humans are the sponsors as well as the victims. White racism is one of the great crimes of history. It is a miracle of grace that black Americans have sustained so much trust in the divine character in the face of black suffering, which appears undeserved and excessive. It has been endured for a long time, is relentless and all-embracing. Black suffering is clearly a result of insensitivity and inhumanity. Why does One who is all-good and all-powerful *permit* one race of men to victimize another race unjustly and incessantly when both are one in his creative and redemptive purposes?

It is native to man to raise the questions Why? and How long? when confronted with the enigma of moral evil as existing and persisting in a good creation providentially guided by a benevolent ruler over the affairs of men. The faith of many has been shaken and even wrecked by the presence and power of evil in their experience. In some sense this is the real God question for a suffering and oppressed people. For a black theologian to raise this question is essential to an entire set of beliefs of black Ameri-

cans. Grappling with this question is not in the nature of
a fad or an intellectual exercise in theological words and
concepts. Let others play a theological word game; but for
the black theologian the God question comes directly out
of the *Lebenswelt* of black victims of white racism in
America and black Africa as well. Theodicy and the God
question are closely associated, as we have observed in
black theology. Suffering is inherent in the human situation. The black man suffers in a double sense. He endures
those experiences of pain inherent in human existence and,
in addition, he endures pain as a victim of inhuman treatment at the hands of the white man.

It is very hazardous to raise the question of theodicy
in the face of the reality of black suffering on any terms
by which one expects an answer in the form of "clear and
distinct ideas." Philosophers, theologians, and moralists
have sought a rational resolution to this problem throughout the history of thought and belief in the East as well as
in the West. The East here refers to the Afro-Asian world.
Africa can no longer be overlooked in such discussions.
The only final answer to the "problem of Job" is some type
of ultimate trust. But this does not preclude a rigorous intellectual quest for some answer to the problem of human
suffering. Here is one instance among others where it is
better to trust God than to put confidence in man. Without
this faith, blacks would not have survived the double dose
of suffering described above.

It is possible for theology to begin with man and move
to God. A careful examination of the human predicament
may indicate the need for God. This does not imply that
God is "invented" because of a profound need for him as
implied by Voltaire. Rather, it is most likely that, as Au-

gustine put it in his *Confessions,* God has made us for himself. And, as John Baillie reminds us in *Our Knowledge of God,* no human soul has been left alone by God. This is true in a personal sense, as the Christian existentialists have taught us. John Macquarrie, in an essay entitled "How Is Theology Possible?" [7] has made a strong case for this approach. He points out that the question of God indicates that man already has some idea of God, however vague or minimal that might be. And, furthermore, according to Macquarrie:

> The question of God arises from man's estrangement from himself, and his ability to bring into unity the polarities of finitude and freedom which constitute his being.[8]

If this can be said regarding man's self-understanding, it must be true in a social sense as well. Since man is a psychosocial being, a person-in-community, his self-understanding is bound up with his social situation. Where humans are oppressed, it may well be that social considerations are prior to questions regarding the self. For most individuals there can be no personal fulfillment where the social environment is too hostile. We are asserting that liberation from oppression is tied up with the humanity of God. A creator and provider God filled with compassion for the disinherited becomes the very cornerstone for theological belief in the context of the black experience.

Thus, we can move logically from a concern for the wholeness of man to the humanity of God. A theology that has as its main focus the plight of an oppressed people must maintain a balance of attention to the wholeness of man and the humanity of God. Blacks have been "hollow men" in a land promising "freedom and justice for all."

Even though such platitudes were written into the principal documents of this republic, there is a real question as to whether the Founding Fathers had in mind the "image of God" in black skin. The history of this country would indicate that in law, custom, and theology, blacks were excluded from the minds of those who penned the liberation documents upon which this nation was based. It will be the very nature of black theology to be iconoclastic regarding *status quo* white theology that denies or ignores the humanity of all men even though it be the theology underpinning contemporary sermons in the White House.

When one examines the volume of collected *White House Sermons,* it is remarkable that black preachers are obvious by their absence. When one is aware that blacks are unusually gifted as orators and preachers, it is clear that the incumbent in the White House, Richard Nixon, is living up to the American tradition regarding the black man. While Billy Graham appears more than once, I am able to identify only one black preacher during the same period. For all his piety, the President does not always see a clear connection between faith and ethics. Again it would be very difficult for a black preacher sensitive about the plight of the black poor to be the kind of prophet who could "tickle the ears" of his audience. Indeed, he could not easily distinguish between the message of the prophets and that of Jesus, as Billy Graham confesses he does. When I made the observation to a lay friend of mine, he remarked: "You don't really expect that black preachers will be invited to the White House, do you?" His point was that they could hardly help becoming true prophets. An Amos in Washington today would be just as unwelcome as Amos of old was in Bethel. Some of his comments on Watergate have indicated that the President needs moral direction. He has compared Watergate with the demonstrations of the 1960's and he has indicated that the Kennedy and Johnson administrations did the same things. His ethical pronouncements have been misguided, confused, and relative. His preachers may have been good priests, but they have been inadequate prophets. For black theologians, religion and politics mix, and faith and ethics are joined. We are concerned about the sharing of power in the interest of human liberation.

I have no final answer for questions relating to the pain and power of God. These are screaming questions when one considers the nature and duration of black oppression in white racist America. Over against this black reality, I will deal with the deep conviction rooted in the Christian creed concerning the humanity of God. That is to say, in spite of all appearances to the contrary, *God does care*. In the language of a black song within the black idiom, *I know he cares!*

I have drawn upon the symbol of the pain of God as used in the theology of Kazoh Kitamori in his work called *Theology of the Pain of God*.[9] This work is "the most self-consciously Japanese of the current theological tendencies in Japan," according to Carl Michalson.[10] This is situational theology. It is an example of rethinking the faith and reformulating it as it speaks to the fundamental human predicament. Buddhism is seen as the Japanese "tradition" in much the same way that Judaism is a fundamental tradition for Pauline theology. Kitamori sees suffering as that which links God, the Christian faith, and Japanese existence. It is obvious that if Shinto, with its world-affirming optimism, had been the foundation for his thought, "pleasure" or "enjoyment" rather than "suffering" would have been the *furoshiki,* or the "wrapping," for Kitamori's theology. The Buddhist gospel of suffering, the disenchantment with Shinto, and the perception of an existentialist among Japanese theologians combine to produce this theology centering in the pain of God.

This is not the only time that "pain" has been employed to refer to "suffering." C. S. Lewis, in his well-known work entitled *The Problem of Pain,* has made this usage familiar in theological circles in the West. What is more important is the manner in which Kitamori uses the symbol of pain in reference to God, and the implication of this for black theology. Black theology is by its very nature concerned with suffering. It is also an attempt at situational theology in the sense that it is rooted in the conditions of black life and the experience of God arises from this context.

Kitamori rightly relates the love of God to the wrath of God. The love and justice of God are properly brought in relation to each other. The God of Amos is the God of Jesus. The God of Jeremiah is the God of Paul. God is one who gets angry over unrighteousness even if his wrath is finally conquered by his love. God is a God who suffers pain even if he has to go outside of himself to do so. He will have nothing to do with a love monism that does not include "the pain caused by God's care for the sinner." [11] God becomes immanent in human misery and the reality of pain. Human pain is a symbol through which man is united to God. He observes that modern theology is deficient because it has no place for this conflict between wrath and love. The cross is an instrument of suffering without teeth. From Schleiermacher to the present, this love monism has been characteristic of Western theology.[12] Black theologians have been schooled in this Western tradition. Even Martin Luther King, Jr., was so captured by the agape motif in the theology of Nygren that he was not able to forge a theological relationship between love and justice, though he was deeply committed to both. The suffering of God for and with man, the unity of love and wrath in God, and the manner in which love overcomes wrath and conquers pain are highly suggestive for reflection in black theology.

Meyer Fortes has discovered notions of fate and destiny as well as justice in West African religions. According to Fortes, the Yoruba, the Bini, and the Dahomeans have a complex system of ancestor worship and a cult of gods or deified beings, together with the notion of destiny. Belief in ancestors is supremely moral and Fortes equates it with belief in "Job's God." The image of the Good Destiny (among the Tallensi) is seen as a simple version of Job's God.[13] Not only is the problem of Job present in African belief, but God is seen as judge. The Yoruba, the Ibo, and others believe that he is a God of judgment. His wrath is incarnate in a divine presence—a divinity of sun and thunder. The Nupe call him *Sokogba,* "God's axe." [14] The question of human suffering, or of God and evil, is universal and takes a rather anxious turn in religious expression among the oppressed. The poet Countee Cullen poses the issue by affirming the goodness and kindness of God on the one hand, and by raising an interesting question of theodicy, of God's justice, on the other. He concludes "Yet Do I Marvel" in this way:

> Yet do I marvel at this curious thing:
> To make a poet black, and bid him sing! [15]

If, as some Biblical literalists would have it, black suffering were the result of some primeval curse, then we could
consider the black man a victim of a second Fall and
excuse white racists for any involvement in the bigotry that
victimizes blacks. But there are neither Biblical nor scien-
tific grounds for such an assumption. Gene Rice has correctly uncovered the abuse of Gen. 9:18–27. He describes
the situation in an essay entitled "The Curse That Never
Was." He writes:

> While Gen. 9:18–27 may well be the most misunderstood
> and abused passage of the Bible, this is not a reflection on
> the Bible itself. Rather, this misuse and abuse attest to
> what perversity the human spirit and intellect can sink and
> with what pains and ingenuity man finds ways to justify to
> himself and to others his sin.[16]

It is clear that racism is sin—a radical evil in the moral
sphere. It is not like the evils that follow natural chaos. It
is not a result brought about by the furies of "earthquake,
wind, and fire." It is a direct result of the perversion of the
human will—of a society of men in white skin setting
themselves up as the lords over men in black skin, often
considering themselves to be righteous in their protection
and care of the black poor. These protectors of the poor
often confuse charity with compassion. They would distinguish between the gift and the giver and thus unwittingly
participate in one of the greatest crimes of history.

It is against the background of our consideration of
racism in these terms and of the suffering of blacks who are
the victims of such racism that we consider the pain of
God. God is actively sharing in the sufferings of the oppressed. God's mediation of his will and his very nature is

in the incarnation. God is revealed in Christ as one who identifies with the lowly, the sinful, and the oppressed to transform their status to one of freedom. God comes to us in Christ, not as a king in royal robes, but as a prince in beggar's garments. He cast his lot with marginal men and women who were not only suffering but rejected as well. In this country with two societies, one black and one white, blacks are the marginal ones. Blacks are like the common people of Jesus' day who first heard the gospel as good news.

God is a God of history. He adopted Israel and entered into her life. His presence and power were a source of strength and guidance for a people traded off between the great powers of the ancient Middle East, a people who experienced throughout the Biblical period as well as through most of history a colonial situation. This God of the exodus is treated in the theology of the Swedish theologian Einar Billing. Gustaf Wingren makes the point this way in his study of Billing:

> Something that had happened in ordinary history—the Exodus—became the spring from which flowed both the biblical confidence for the future, that is, the eschatological hope, and the biblical tranquility in regard to the course of the world, that is, the doctrine of creation. Faith continually receives strength from this event.[17]

This God who was a benevolent and provident God for Israel comes to us as the Liberator where he reveals himself as the Lord. But the God who reveals himself as Lord is also the Suffering Servant. He entered the marketplace, traveled the byways, and mingled with the "wretched of the earth." This God is the source of the Christian faith.

In Christ he makes himself fully known. Albert C. Outler writes of God:

> God's unswerving pursuit of His goals for man in the midst of the turmoils of human history is an even more striking proof of His providence and total investment than any form of aloofness could ever be. For there is never any question as to who has the initiative in nature and history and the provisions for the mystery of salvation are what they are by the elect counsel and design of the Most High, beside whom there is no other.[18]

Outler rightly rejects that Christian theodicy which is bound by immutability and impassibility. He asserts that in Biblical terms God's freedom does not require "ontic barriers for His self-defense." He continues:

> Because He really is sovereign, He truly is free to allow evil as the dark shadow of corrupted good and yet sovereign to veto its final triumph. The sovereignty that reigns unchallenged is not as absolute as the sovereignty that accepts the risks of involvement and yet provides appropriate resources for human fulfillment even in the depths of tragedy.

Douglas J. Hall has noted that Christianity on this continent, with the possible exception of the faith of black people, has never been significantly influenced by a theology of the cross.[19] Perhaps a *theologia crucis* is the hallmark of black religion, but in black religion one would be ill advised to identify this theology of the cross with pietism only, for it is a faith for survival and meaning involving a political ethic. According to Hall the *theologia crucis* has been absorbed by a *theologia gloriae*. The cross has been co-opted by a triumphalism. The "yes" of Easter overcomes the "no" of the empty tomb. But Christians, ac-

cording to Hall, must witness to a Christ in whom men
can really find their own suffering reflected.[20] This is the
only way men will get to know of the pain of God and see
his humanity revealed.

Anyone who seriously reflects upon Du Bois' *The Souls
of Black Folk* or his "A Litany at Atlanta" will understand
the agony of blacks and their spiritual strivings from the
depths.

> Listen to us, Thy children: our faces dark with doubt are
> made a mockery in Thy sanctuary. With uplifted hands we
> front Thy heaven, O God, crying:
> *We beseech Thee to hear us, good Lord!* [21]

It is a fact of history that the Atlanta Riot of 1906 reveals the utter moral confusion of white Christians and
their theology. In the name of social reform, preachers as
well as politicians supported riots, lynching, and mass ter-
rorism. A general slaughter of blacks, or "genocide," became a real possibility. Meanwhile white preachers noted
that women and whiskey were the temptations to avoid.
When black men began the rape of white women, no means
of death was too brutal to give satisfaction to the white
community. These men were considered brutes and fiends,
for they had committed a crime against white women, who
were seen as the most beautiful and the purest women in
history. Anything that was done to the black man was supported by the will of God and the laws of men, which
meant white supremacy.[22] It is against this background that
Du Bois raises the theodicy question. Samuel F. Yette in
The Choice (1971) paints a picture of the black man's
survival in America which is almost as bleak as the Atlanta
situation of 1906. Yette, now a professor of journalism,

was dismissed from *Newsweek* shortly after he published this explosive work. His work is well researched and well documented. Much of what he said has been reinforced by events throughout the country. The theodicy question for blacks must reflect the black reality in this society.

Not only blacks, but others, such as Herman Melville and Harriet Beecher Stowe, have described racism as "the American national sin." [23] White theology may be able to ignore these facts, but from the black perspective there can be no meaningful understanding of God which does not take seriously this stark reality—the unmerited suffering of blacks in a society saturated with white racism, both personal and institutional. While it is important for black theologians to consider the classical statements of theodicy, it is most important for them to rethink the issue in terms of Jewish holocaust theology, liberation theology, and the black experience of religion. [24]

In *The Creation of the World and Other Business,* a play by Arthur Miller, Lucifer engages God in conversation. At first Lucifer does most of the talking. He would convince God that they should work together. According to Lucifer, if good and evil stood together, there would be no war. Without absolute righteousness, there would be no war. Lucifer assures God that if they could stand together, there would be a second paradise. But in the end, God replies that he will accept the odds rather than accept help from unrighteousness. According to Miller, Lucifer is consigned to hell. When Lucifer extends his hand, God rejects it, saying: "Never! Never, never, never!" Then Lucifer threatens to take the world. God replies: "And if ever you do, I will burn it. . . . For I am the Lord and the Lord is good and only good!" [25]

It has been the conviction of black Christians that in spite of all the social evil they have experienced at the hands of whites, God is good and only good. This is why blacks can sing in one breath, "Nobody knows the trouble I've seen," and in the next, "Glory, hallelujah!" We know that "trouble don't last always," for God is good, just, righteous, and merciful.

It is in Jesus' cry of dereliction, "My God, my God, why hast thou forsaken me?" that we observe the pain at the heart of God. We know that the Biblical God is not the god of Aristotle, a remote abstraction, an unmoved absolute, but that he is one who shares our griefs and bears our sorrows. He is a personal God of infinite compassion and suffering love. He identifies with those who bear the mark of oppression. He is not blind and deaf to black suffering. God "sees all we do and hears all we say." His requirements are love, justice, humility, and mercy. The assurance that God enters into our life with the full measure of his suffering love as manifest on the cross is a source of great comfort and strength for an oppressed people. This understanding of God brings not merely resources to endure hardship but a determination to seek freedom from all forms of bondage. God has identified with their liberating struggle.

God as power is a crucial concept for black theology, as it is also for a theology of liberation. Power is an important concept as we can see from the Christian's confrontation with secular power and power structures today. At a time when there is "dirty politics" and the obvious abuse of power, it would appear rather unholy to suggest that Christians get involved in politics. But for an oppressed people, survival and meaning are bound up with the sharing of power. Religion and politics are already mixed, but they are "mixed" against our welfare and our humanity. A proper theological understanding of power in God and among men is basic to a black political theology. A powerless people being crushed by the ruthless abuse of power in a racist society needs a Christian understanding of God as power. Indeed, after Watergate all Americans need to question the nature of piety on the Potomac and deal with the theological and moral issues surrounding the nature, use, and abuse of power.

Power is deeply rooted in the Judeo-Christian understanding of God. The Bible speaks often of God as power. He is omnipotent, almighty, and hence the ultimate source of power (John 19:11; Rom. 13:1). Power belongs to God (Ps. 62:11). Various divine activities are explained by God's power. God's power is likewise associated with his revelation. God, however, enters into self-limitation insofar as power is concerned in order to share power with men and grant them the freedom of selfhood and the responsibility of persons.

God exercises power in creation and in his reconciling work. God is the One who "lets be," as John Macquarrie puts it. Creation is a manifestation of God's almightiness. In the manner of his loving and judging men we have further evidence of God's power. Power is the means through which he accomplishes his purpose as creator, redeemer, and sanctifier.

Power is the support for his sovereignty. All other powers are subject to God as the final source of power. As absolute power, self-limited only by the balance in his nature and the integrity of his character, he opposes the idolatry of power in all history and creation. Because God is sovereign power, there can be no divine rights of earthly rulers, kings, prime ministers, or presidents. All human power is under God. Paul, who declared government to be ordained of God, should have distinguished between what God permits and what he ordains. The sovereignty of God excludes the absolute power of the state and of the people. All human power is limited by divine power and eternal law. A theology of power in Christian perspective must acknowledge the primacy of the power of God and at the same time categorically reject all absolutizing of any form of human power. The Christian still owes his ultimate allegiance to God. Ultimate loyalty and obedience is to God. We can have no "godfather," for our ultimate confidence and obedience is due to our heavenly Father, who is a God of power. This God of power is a God who delivers the oppressed from all forms of human bondage. This God challenges all oppressive earthly power:

> Listen!—Listen!
> All you sons of Pharaoh.
> Who do you think can hold God's people
> When the Lord God himself has said,
> Let my people go? [26]

God does share his power with men. Power is a gift from God to man. Power in itself is neutral. It may be used to create or to destroy, depending upon the purpose for which it is employed. Power, like freedom, can be exercised to bless or to curse. Man as man is invested with power. He has the power to hate, but he also has the power to love; he has the power to do evil, but also the power to do good! Man has power to be free, but it is often used to enslave himself and others. The proper use of power is for freedom, justice, and righteousness.

The Hebrew word for God, *El*, or *Elohim*, is apparently derived from a root meaning "to be strong." The Hebrew proper name for God, "Jehovah," or "Yahweh," seems to have expressed originally the idea of independent power or existence. This meaning is conveyed by the words "I AM THAT I AM," with which God introduced himself to Moses (Ex. 3:13–15). Divine omnipotence is stressed in the New Testament as well as the Old. The reason is a practical one. The all-powerfulness of God inspires personal trust. God is equal to all our needs. Jesus said, "All things are possible with God" (Mark 10:27), and Paul speaks of God as one "that is able to do exceeding abundantly above all that we ask or think" (Eph. 3:20). Only omnipotence can guarantee redemption. God is a promise-keeping God. Faith can become an actual triumph over the world because God is a God of power.

For a black political theology, God as power is important. God as power is indispensable for a believing trust in the promises of God. It is important for an oppressed people to have the assurance that God is the only absolute source of power. Such an assurance is necessary in order for the powerless to maintain a semblance of hope. We have overcome because we have trusted in a God of power who has brought strength out of weakness. God as power is essential to black political theology also for the reason that racism is a social evil that is built into the power structures of our society. We need a God of power to oppose the institutional racism of our society, which robs a whole people of their humanity. Where there is a power of evil, there must be a greater power for good if the victims of the evil power are to be set free. God as power is, by faith, the black man's hope of liberation.

Power is essential for the moral integrity of God. Goodness, love, righteousness, and holiness are components of the divine character. Even imagination is essential to the fullness of the life of God. God's love is imaginatively limitless. Love needs to be expressed through imagination. Concern is more effective when expressed thus. If we use an image or a likeness of a suffering human, we are able to arouse the imagination of other men at a deeper level than if we use statistics, which are often cold and inaccurate, depending upon who is doing the interpretation. But when people's imagination is aroused to the extent that they really feel empathy with the oppressed, their compassion is aroused and they are able to express their concern more deeply. This brief look at imagination as an attribute of God indicates the need for black theologians to share with other theologians fresh ways of understanding God, based on their experience of him. But a black political theology has a special mission. It is to be a theology of power.

We need to know that everlasting love in God is sustained by absolute power. God's love will prevail because God's power is unchallenged ultimately by all opposing power. God is the Lord of history and will have the last word. This knowledge is crucial as we oppose white racism, for the white declaration of black inferiority is one of the crimes of history that cuts against the grain of the purpose and sovereignty of God. The moral nature of God and his almighty power are in opposition to inhumanity and injustice. Because of the very goodness of God, racism, which is a form of idolatry, is being opposed by the sovereign Power in the universe. An understanding of God as power, then, is crucial. Any theological stance that ignores the cruciality of power as a sustaining support for the moral integrity of God is not likely to be worthy of acceptance by any oppressed people when they reach the level of longing for liberation. Power supports but does not supplant love and justice in God.

Black political theology is rooted in a new consciousness, a new self-understanding on the part of blacks. In the quest of personal worth and peoplehood apart from full acceptance into the Euro-American culture, belief in God as power is important. White women are seeking a personal sense of worth apart from their husbands. One young white woman indicated to me that her understanding of God had changed. She did not know her father. She indicated that the "motherhood" of God would "turn her on." She was concerned with an understanding of God that would liberate her as an individual. Blacks need an understanding of God that will liberate their people, and so do perhaps two thirds of the human race, who are oppressed in one way or another.

We have for a long period been systematically excluded from the American mainstream. We had had to find meaning for our lives in a permanent counter culture or subculture. Blacks have found hope in the assurance that the God who cares is also able. The God of love is also a God of power. He is the God of the exodus, of the exile and the kingdom, the God of the cross and the resurrection. This is the stuff of a personal faith that is satisfying and sustaining. It is likewise the basis for a new sense of peoplehood. God as power implies that a people in bondage may be delivered and a people in exile may be restored. This is the faith of our black fathers, living still, in spite of lash, dogs, and cattle prods. We have forged a trust out of the belief that the God of love and justice is a God of power.

Black political theology has to deal with power structures within "immoral society." We are the victims of a cancer in a whole social order that is destroying our people, robbing them of their potential and consigning thousands of our youth to an early death, to long prison terms and wasted lives. As black churchmen and theologians, we love this people. Our understanding of God must include his concern and ours for what America has done and is doing to a whole people. A few blacks believe they have made it and these have become part of the problem. What we need is a solution—an answer for those who cry from the depths of misery, Why?

Black political theology, therefore, must approach the question of God in view of the need for answers to deep personal and social concerns of black people. To conceive of God as power is not merely good social psychology but good theology as well. God is the Lord of history. Racism, which has chained and penalized a people, declaring them to be inherently inferior in the manner in which the Creator made them, is a serious theological problem, which needs to be tackled at the base level of theological ethics. Racism is not a natural evil; it is a moral evil. Human beings in white skin have played God in their mistreatment of the brother in black skin. It is essential that all Bible-thumping white racists confront the fact that they have invested everything in "a curse that never was" and that the real curse is the idolatry of race, which has enslaved and dehumanized not only the black man but themselves. Understanding God as the one who lets be, as creator, redeemer, and judge, in all creation and in all history, is essential as a theological foundation upon which to oppose this type of systematic racism. Such white racism has made hopelessness and self-hatred a self-fulfilling prophecy for far too many blacks. A black political theology sees God as a God of love and justice whose power is sufficient to oppose every structure that denies the humanity of the black poor and all the oppressed among humankind.

God is a Father who suffers with his people. He gets angry at unrighteousness. He is concerned about the liberation of individuals, but as a God of history he is concerned about the deliverance of peoples as well. This God of love and wrath enters into our lives and controls the destiny of men and nations. His love overcomes his wrath, but he balances his love with his justice and his power. Gardner C. Taylor, himself a prince of the pulpit, introduces a volume containing sermons by his fellow black preachers with the following remarks:

> In this volume will be found those "angles of vision" of the Scriptures and of human life not immediately and easily available to any preachers except those who are part of a disillusioned and disinherited community. Likewise, there will be seen here again and again a vivid imagery and a stubborn, strong, and splendid faith in a God whose power is more than match for men's evil structures of oppression and who supremely illustrated His power to overcome at Calvary.[27]

5

Jesus Means Freedom

Joseph Washington in *Black Religion* referred to black religion as "Jesusology." [1] There is no proper theological understanding of the person and work of Christ, he observes. Blacks relate only to the life and ministry of Jesus. It is too much to expect Washington, then and perhaps even now, to note the theological point that blacks were making in exalting the earthly Jesus. Howard Thurman had made the point rather well in his *Jesus and the Disinherited*. [2] Washington was so observant of the unorthodox nature of Thurman's message that the real thrust of what Thurman was saying about Jesus did not occur to him. Thurman was saying that an oppressed people can behold the human face of God only through the Jesus who as a man lived the very life of God. Washington did not comprehend the reason why blacks who appeared to be "playing church" did not go insane or take their own lives under such great hardships, and neither did he attempt to explain why they gave Jesus the title of power, "King Jesus." [3] It is too much to expect an anticipation of the black power movement in the early 1960's, but it is well that we now reflect on the same themes.

Albert Cleage, who came to public notice during the crest of the black power movement as an exponent of the "black Messiah," [4] has been referred to as "the prophet of the black nation." Cleage was greatly inspired by Marcus Garvey, "the black Moses," and by S. G. F. Brandon's study of *Jesus and the Zealots*.[5] Cleage sees Jesus as a religious revolutionary who was interested in the salvation and growth of a nation. The individual religion of "the blood of the Lamb" belongs to the apostle Paul. Whites converted blacks to Paul's religion, and, according to Cleage, Paul "was one of the biggest Uncle Toms in history." The mission of the black church is to rediscover the the religion of Jesus.[6] In a more recent study, Cleage has this to say:

> The theological basis for the gospel of liberation can be found in the life and teachings of Jesus. Not in His death, but in His life. . . . God reconciled men unto Himself in the life and teachings of Jesus which gave men a new conception of human dignity and inspired them to fight to be men instead of slaves.[7]

My negative criticisms of Cleage's thought have already been stated. On the positive side, I believe him to be essentially correct in stressing the identification of Jesus with the oppressed, aiding them in their liberation struggle.

The quest of black theology is not for a "gentle Jesus, meek and mild." We have had a double dose of spiritual aspirin. Africans say that the white missionaries exchanged this Jesus and the Bible for their land and resources. Black Americans lost their freedom. No sentimental Jesusology

will do. Few blacks are members of the new Jesus movement, with its interest in personal salvation and life after
death. Racism has already "deprogrammed" the black
man. What we seek is an introduction to the "political
Jesus." We do not seek to make Jesus a captive of black
culture as we reject the cultural captivity of the Jesus de-
picted by Euro-Americans. Such a Jesus would only give
endorsement to the oppressed condition of black folk in the
same manner in which "the white, Americanized Christ"
has sprinkled holy water upon the "God and country" syndrome of "whiteanity." Neither do we desire to "iconize"
Jesus as a representative of the transcendent and invisible
world alone. No theology that seeks to write a revolutionary manifesto into its creeds with liberation from oppression in view can accept fondly the iconization of Jesus.

Black theology cannot accept either the Jesus who pre-
serves the American way of life or the Jesus of the counter
culture. Jesus is not, for us, the world's greatest business
organizer, the chairman of the biggest board of all. He is
not the bringer of wealth, peace of mind, or Consciousness
III. He is not the one who is uniquely suited to fit our
mood. He is not a super athlete. Neither is he a societal
dropout, a political subversive, a guerrilla fighter complete
with submachine gun.[8] In other words, Jesus must not be
locked into a given cluster of political and cultural per-
ceptions. We seek a Christ *above* culture who is at the
same time at work *in* culture and history for redemptive
ends—setting free the whole person, mind, soul, and body.
Jesus speaks to the need of blacks to be whole persons in
a society in which they are "mere faces in the crowd."
Jesus also speaks to a need for peoplehood. He brings hope
and assurance to a people "seeking some place to be at

home." Jesus was a Jew, but he was and is "the desire of all nations." The quest for humanity leads us through personal wholeness and peoplehood to a community in which all are brothers and even *heirs*.

There have been recent attempts to deny the classical Christological assertion that the Jesus of history is the Christ of faith.[9] This tendency to modernize Jesus has frequently been sponsored by those who have done intense study on original sources. Therefore their conclusions, though arbitrary, seem to carry the weight of authority. For instance, observe John Allegro's "sacred mushroom" Jesus. Allegro claims that Jesus was the high priest of a drug culture in his day.[10] More recently Morton Smith suggested that Jesus developed a baptismal rite as a magician and took his pupils on a "trip." This experience gave his followers supernatural powers and freed them from the law. The rite, based upon ancient erotic magic, included spirit possession and sexual union. Jesus is pictured as being at the center of a libertine circle.[11]

Where do we go from here? "They have taken away my Lord and I know not where they have laid him." This modernizing is evidence of the bankruptcy of both the "quest" and the "new quest" for the historical Jesus. Such relevancy in Christology is a dead-end street. One almost longs for an otherworldly, eschatological Jesus and "Kingdom ethics" grasped only by a blind leap of faith. Surely Jesus must be lifted up above the cesspool where much careful archaeological and exegetical study has laid him. It is almost comforting to read again of the Barthian Jesus as the Word of God or of the Tillichian existential Christ. We tire of reading in the popular press of what new evidence scholars have dug up which cuts away at the very foundations of belief in Christ. Christian humanists are undermined as much as Christian theists. The humanity as well as the divinity of Christ is being questioned. He is not *very* God, but neither is he *very* man. He is no longer savior, but neither is he perfect man or a superb moral example of man at his highest and best. Both the moral influence theory and the substitutionary theory of the atonement have been undercut. And yet it is the interpretation of the evidence rather than the scholarly evidence itself which is to be seriously questioned.

Henry Nicholson, a black writer who manages to present a "colorless" book at this time of black awareness, insists that Jesus is *really* dead. He accepts the skepticism of his white sources and teachers. And yet he tries to make a strong case for the humanity of Jesus, especially in his concern that religion be a "concerned responsibility." Nicholson writes:

> To reject the fact of Jesus' death is to virtually forfeit the life and energy of current society in general.[12]

He wants a religion that is thinkable, speakable, and livable, that is in no way bound up with an immortalized Jesus. He sees belief in a living Jesus as being lost in the past. What we need is a faith that is updated and alive today. He fears that the "God is dead" people are trying to set up a "Jesus is God" substitute.

This book is a great disappointment to a writer of black theology. Nicholson is obviously not a specialist in theology by training or experience. He is not "thinking black." He does not reflect upon his subject out of the black religious experience. He does not ask what understanding of Jesus has informed and supported black people through the dark

night of black suffering. Neither does he provide us with
the type of political Jesus that relates to our present liberation struggle. He is too busy paying his dues to white
scholars and is yet not fully aware that the "death of God"
movement is dead and has never been alive insofar as
blacks are concerned. Even Bultmann would not abandon
the death-resurrection event. Good Friday and Easter are
the essence of the faith. Nowhere in Christendom is faith
in Jesus as the living Lord more present and powerful than
in the black church. Without this faith we could not have
survived and neither would we be able to act for our liberation in the present nor hope for a brighter future.

As a black theologian I am not happy with Cleage's
Jesus who is black, alive, and well, but I am less enchanted
with Nicholson's Jesus who is white and no longer with us.
It remains for us to look briefly at James Cone's Christology. In Cone we meet a bright mind at work on the proper
Biblical and theological sources but reflecting upon the
black condition. He sees the black Christ thus:

> The Black Christ is He who threatens the structure of
> evil as seen in white society, rebelling against it, thereby
> becoming the embodiment of what the black community
> knows that it must become. Because He has become black
> as we are, we now know what black empowerment is.[13]

It would take considerable time to criticize fairly Cone's
Christology. I admire the manner in which he "thinks
black" in his presentation while forging a profound theological statement. I can identify in spirit with Cleage and
Cone, but Cone's position appears sounder and is based
upon more convincing evidence. As one who maintains a
deep appreciation for revelation and humanism in my theo-

logical perspective, I am unhappy with the obvious Barthian hangup implicit in Cone. While a black theologian may not be bound completely by the structures of traditional theology, he needs a consistent way of moving from the Christ of faith to the Jesus of history. In other words, there should be a logical relationship between faith and ethics in the manner in which the Christological statement is made. The kerygmatic Christ of Cone is accessible only by a leap of faith. He is the Christ of salvation history, a central figure in the theology of the Word. Only those who accept this Christocentric understanding of theology can accept his interpretation of even the black Christ, who is his version of the Jesus of history. Even so the real problem in Cone is the lack of direction from his Christology to his ethics. Since his entire theology is Christocentric, his ethics stem from his Christology. This is where the rub comes. Preston Williams is concerned about the lack of empirical evidence to support Cone's ethics. It bothers Williams that Cone does not invest much in blacks winning their liberation struggle.[14]

My own concern is more theological. Cone does not see any relation between the teaching and example of Jesus and his so-called black Christ, who is involved in the black liberation struggle. We are not to raise the question, What would Jesus do? for his situation was so different from ours. To take this position is to leave the troops of the black liberation army, already confused, in a state of total moral confusion. In political matters it would be well for them to turn from theology altogether to those ideologies and movements in the cause of black liberation which offer direction and definite programs. But where would this leave the black church, the only institutional giant at our

disposal? The black church needs a theology of social
change and political action. Christ the center of our faith
is the focus of such theology. Surely black theology must
provide the understanding in faith and ethics adequate for
the liberation mission of the black church. The reconception of an adequate Christology for a black political theology is perhaps the primary challenge awaiting the black
theologian.

While black scholars read, analyze, and assess what is
going on in their fields of specialization, they have a much
more urgent task as they look at Jesus. The question,
"What do you think of the Christ?" and "What shall I do
with Jesus who is called Christ?" are at the center of our
quest. Jesus means freedom. His is the Liberator. This indicates that we cannot abandon either the Jesus of history
or the Christ of faith. We need both. If the evidence is not
conclusive to support our claims, neither is the evidence
conclusive against our claim. Even Cullmann, who rejects
any kind of this-worldly, revolutionary understanding of
Jesus and his mission, asks us to accept his conclusions
mainly on faith.[15] After I had read Cullmann and weighed
his evidence and pondered his conclusions, my initial reaction was that if Jesus were *really* as otherworldly as he
makes him, I too would become a Muslim. Fortunately,
there are other possibilities for me as a theologian.

A powerless people living under oppressed conditions
needs to know that things can be otherwise—that a more
humane and just order is possible. Our understanding of
the Messiah-Savior is that he is a part of this liberation
struggle of the oppressed. Being aware of our own lack
and the insensitivity of others to our claims for social
justice, we are assured that "the Man for others" has the

integrity and the power to establish justice in the earth. We are concerned with man's inhumanity to man. Thus the entry of God into history in the incarnation has a vital message for us. Those who have come of age, post-Christian men of the technological age, dwellers in the secular city, may live as if God were not and make it on their own. But a people of adversity need to know that God *is* and that he is *gracious*. We are not prepared to say: God is dead, and long live Jesus. We see Jesus as the chief revealer of the very life of God. The Jesus of history is precious in the eyes of the oppressed. All the "wretched of the earth" who come to know him bask in the light of his presence. The oppressed thrive in the moral influence and power of the incarnate Lord. Those who have been victims of such gross inhumanity as slavery and discrimination have difficulty with belief in the inherent goodness of man. We have the need for more than a moral example in Jesus. We need a savior as well. Not the Lamb of God who pays it all and saves us only one by one. We understand him to be one who is able to work *in* and *through* us to will and to do beyond all that we are able to ask or think on our own. We understand him to be one who can express compassion for multitudes and weep over a whole nation. The Jesus of history for blacks is one who brings deliverance and hope to men and nations. We reject the "man on his own" thesis of Ernst Bloch. Our trust is in the One who called sinners to repentance and ate with the outcasts of his day.

If Jesus is only human, the black masses are without hope through their faith. These are they who must reach up to touch bottom. Their tragic plight from generation to generation is constant and their suffering cries for relief. To follow the exalted moral example of Jesus under such conditions does not appear to be a "possible impossibility"—only an "impossibility." The ceiling rather than the sky is the limit of their vision and aspirations. The walls of the dark ghetto form the circle of their experience. Pimps, prostitutes, ex-convicts and con men represent the "success stories" for the young. The "bad nigger," who beats the System, who outshoots and outcons the worst white gangsters, is the "moral hero" of the new black films that are popular in the inner cities today. In order to make it in the movies, our best actors and actresses are falling for the new stereotypes of prostituting themselves for fame and fortune. Black youths are being exploited at the ticket office. Black teen-agers live vicariously through the parade of the "bad nigger" on the screen. What is remarkable is the silence of the black church as black youths are being exploited and as money that could be used for the empowerment of black people is being garnered into the coffers of the white theater owners. These owners profit from the filth being fed in large doses to our youth, who need a healthier diet to make them whole.

This society is so ordered that those who belong to the black masses cannot make it morally or legally. And yet society lures all toward the American Dream. The Jesus of history who cast his lot with the oppressed has special relevance to the black situation. He judges us not by what we are, but by our potential. He meets us where we are and enables us to be transformed into his likeness. This is good news. But this message must be translated into concrete terms. The word must become flesh. Goods and services must be at the top of the black agenda. We must be concerned about the politics of Jesus. For the black poor, Jesus means freedom.

A black scholar who was doing research on black religion inquired of me as to whether I had abandoned my earlier stance on Christology. He referred to my Jesus of history and Christ of faith formula, which I owe to Donald Baillie's *God Was in Christ*. Since this is a Euro-American position, he wondered if I had begun to "think black." His concern was to seek a more authentic "African" Christology. My reply was an emphatic reaffirmation of my earlier position. He was visibly shaken and obviously disappointed. My friend had assumed that I had grown beyond this view to a greater black awareness as he saw it. He was not impressed with my distinction between the *form* and the *substance* of Christology. Here it seems wise to clarify my perspective for those who are still open for dialogue.

The meaning of any Christological statement has to be appropriated in a cultural context. But this cultural milieu is the medium and not the message—it is form and not content. Earlier we mentioned that E. Bolaji Idowu, the Nigerian, was shocked into reality as he listened to a film in which Jesus spoke "American" rather than "British" English. He realized that Nigerians need a Christ who speaks Yoruba and other Nigerian languages, and who speaks redemptively to Nigerians in their cultural setting. Vincent Harding's critique of the "white, Americanized Christ" is well known. A Christological statement that is ethnic and indigenous must deal with these considerations.

We must distinguish between the *esse* and the *bene esse* of Christology. The essence or the substance of our Christology must be set apart, for clarity, from the structure or form in which it is presented. The affirmation of faith in the person and work of Christ is centered in the *esse* of Christology. There is an ecumenical consensus as to what this is, at least in mainstream Protestantism. The psycho-cultural and historical experiences through which the message is appropriated provide the form which the *bene esse* of Christology will take. The gospel of Jesus Christ receives its drive, power, and effectiveness from those who listen and obey. Black awareness, drawing upon the whole history of Afro-American religious experience, provides the *bene esse* of Christology in black theology. The *esse* is still the universal Word. Christ is Lord of *each* people, but he is also Lord of all. Particularity and universality, Jewishness and the desire of all nations are united in this reconception of Christology in the context of black awareness and black power. Jesus is *with* every people, but he is not *of* any people. The Redeemer is also the Judge. His judgment is more than an internal cultural criticism. He judges *in* history from beyond history. He stands outside and above black culture as well as within it. This is crucial if his relation to a people is to redeem and transform them. He seeks "to make all things new" in our personhood and within our peoplehood.

A favorite hymn in the black church is "What a Friend We Have in Jesus!" Jesus has long been considered by blacks as a divine friend. White fundamentalists have also had a similar appreciation for Jesus. Now the "Jesus people" have fallen in love with him. But since the total life situation for whites is different, and this is especially true of middle-class "Jesus freaks," the understanding of the person and place of Jesus is different. Whites, generally, have a personal and otherworldly understanding of Jesus. The motto "Jesus saves" implies believers' preparation to meet God after death, one by one. Jesus keeps you from burning in hell or he brings peace of mind. Once you know Jesus as your Savior, you evangelize by ringing doorbells and passing out leaflets about heaven and hell. Because Jesus brings inner peace, beyond what has been experienced in permissive sex or on drug trips, Jesus turns you on. Faith can work a miracle; therefore, we are not gainsaying what radical changes have taken place in the lives of those who have accepted Jesus with this understanding. The problems and conditions of life for blacks are so social in character that more than personal religion is needed. The meaning of Jesus Christ for blacks is different.

While we have often bought this personal and otherworldly version of Jesusology, we have internalized it in our own way. We are an oppressed race. We are poor, uneducated, unemployed, and burdened by "the troubles of this world." We are "a blues people," as Imamu Amiri Baraka so aptly puts it. James Cone is correct: "To be black is to be blue." To be black is to fight constantly for survival and dignity when the odds are against you. To be black is to know troubles and to learn to live with sorrows as well as joys. We sing "Jesus Paid It All," "Take All the World and Give Me Jesus," and the like, too often. Jesus means spiritual aspirin for the headaches and heartaches of black existence in a racist society. Jesusology is escapism, quietism, an opiate for black people received in church on Sunday morning. A good dose will last all week. Since few blacks, poor or middle class, can afford psychiatrists, we have Jesus. But, for blacks enduring great hardships and sufferings, even the sedative quality of Jesusology has been understood in such a manner as to bring meaning and hope into an otherwise unbearable existence.

Ernst Käsemann in *Jesus Means Freedom* criticizes those who, in the name of respectable orthodoxy, are silent about the inhumanity tolerated and promoted by Christians. They do not hear the voice of him who asks, What have you done (or not done) to me in my brother? [16] Co-humanity is what he actually lived, gave, and demanded, according to Käsemann.[17] He sees Jesus as making co-humanity possible by relating it to the reign of God.[18] Käsemann concludes that Jesus was a "liberal," uniting devotion and loving concern for the human condition:

> He was unique in that He remained, lived and died, acted and spoke, in the freedom of being a child of God. The freedom of God's children, who were lost but are now reconciled and recalled, is His revelation, His glory, gift, and claim. Since Him and through Him the freedom of God's children has been the true symbol of the gospel and the final criterion for all who call themselves Christians.[19]

In his birth, life, and death on a cross, Jesus cast his lot with the oppressed. This is why James Cone, speaking symbolically, insists that in America Jesus is black, for Jesus is the oppressed One. Through Jesus we come to know the humanity of God. Karl Barth of Basel wrote concerning the "humanity of God" at the end of his long career. It took this theologian, whose theology is Christocentric and who exalted the otherness and transcendence of God, almost a half century to discover the humanity of God. But the humblest black Christian has always known the humanity of God through Jesus.

Another concern of black theology is the nature of the ministry of Jesus. Was it quietistic or political? Was Jesus a quietistic announcer of the coming Kingdom or was he a revolutionary? Was he otherworldly or this-worldly in his ethics? Did he have anything to say against evil here and now or was he only concerned about the eschatological future? Oscar Cullmann has written an intense work to assure us that Jesus was not a radical. What he means is that Jesus was not a Zealot and did not use or endorse violence as a method to oppose evil. He seems to insist also that Jesus was not really involved or concerned about social change here and now, for his Kingdom was future and not of this world. He does make some allowance for the difference between his situation and ours since the Kingdom did not come in its fullness as he had expected. What Cullmann allows by way of implication from the ethics of Jesus is what may best be described as "personal ethics." [20] Jesus had no perception of "public ethics" and did not give us direction in the fight against what Tillich called the "demonic" and what Reinhold Niebuhr referred to as "immoral society." It is here that I am in total agreement with James Cone:

> With all due respect to erudite New Testament scholars and the excellent work that has been done in this field, I cannot help but conclude that they are "straining out a gnat and swallowing a camel"! It is this kind of false interpretation that leads to the oppression of the poor. As long as the oppressor can be sure that the gospel does not threaten his social, economic and political security, he can enslave men in the name of Christ.[21]

According to Brandon in *Jesus and the Zealots,* we must take seriously the fact that the crucifixion was a Roman form of capital punishment. The fact that Jesus "suffered under Pontius Pilate" indicates that sedition against the Roman government in Judea was the reason for his death. Theologians, including New Testament scholars, have provided a theological interpretation of the crucifixion while overlooking the historical problem. Even the New Testament documents are mainly apologetic. According to Brandon, Jesus died as a revolutionary against oppressive Roman power. Brandon believes that a careful investigation of the Zealot movement will enable one to understand better the historical Jesus. Jesus "chose a Zealot for an apostle . . . , died crucified between two men, probably Jewish resistance fighters, who had challenged Rome's sovereignty over Israel." [22] In the examination of Cullmann and Brandon one gets a look at the divided mind of some of the white scholars of whom Cone spoke.

John Howard Yoder presents a "messianic pacifism" based upon his Christology. The problem is not that there is no basis for a social ethic in the gospel, but that we choose to ignore it because of the radical demands it places upon us. He rejects attempts to spiritualize and individualize the gospel. The cross results from a moral clash between the powers in society. Jesus called into question the prevailing social order. Believers must expect the cross as the price of social nonconformity as they participate in the reality of the Kingdom in a world of unbelief.[23] Yoder believes that Jesus calls us as members of a new community based upon nonresistant love. The society provides for a new way for men to live together in which they are forgiven and in which violence is dealt with through innocent suffering. This new community thus provides a new way to deal with corrupt society. "Nonresistance is right, not because it works, but because it anticipates the tri-

umph of the Lamb that was slain." [24] According to Yoder,
Jesus did not bring an admonition to be concerned about
the political; rather, Jesus brought a definite form of politics by calling men to participation in the nonresistant
community.[25]

James Cone and I sat through a session with several
theologians on the East Coast. There were obvious differences of opinion on the nature of the ministry of Jesus. As
black theologians we were agreed that while erudite white
scholars may argue the matter pro and con, the oppressed
will accept Jesus as a political messiah. We will take seriously the manifesto of Nazareth:

> The Spirit of the Lord is upon me,
> because he has anointed me to preach good
>   news to the poor.
> He has sent me to proclaim release to the captives
> and recovering of sight to the blind,
> to set at liberty those who are oppressed,
> to proclaim the acceptable year of the Lord.
>   (*Luke 4:18–19,* RSV.)

The question as to how we reconcile the scandal of particularity with the universalism of the gospel is another
important consideration for black theology. If Jesus is
with the oppressed, the disinherited, the man in black skin,
how then will he save the privileged, the rich, the oppressor
in white skin? Doesn't the theological formulation of the
black Messiah automatically become racist? If so, what
has happened to the fatherhood of God and the brotherhood of man? What does the gospel of Jesus Christ say to
blacks who are no longer among the poor? Many of these
questions will be rejected by blacks as being the wrong
questions, at the wrong time, and by the wrong theologian.

A black theology which asserts that reconciliation is an ultimate Christian consideration cannot escape some of these hard questions. These are representative questions that many Christians of both races are asking as they sincerely seek direction through the maze of social conflict caused by racism.

The gospel is both universal and particular. Jesus is the Savior of each and the Lord of all. Howard Thurman, in a conversation with the author, made this penetrating observation: "I cannot escape the 'Jewness' of Jesus." But as we have indicated, Jesus is for all men. His love is personal and individual. He numbers the very hairs of our heads. He reached into a teeming multitude and healed a helpless cripple. Each person is precious in his sight. At the same time he looked with compassion upon the multitude. But it is because he loves each of us that he loves all of us. He could not love all without loving each. It was possible for me to identify with the hungry children who clung to me like leeches in Calcutta, Cairo, and Lagos because I am the father of small children. By loving a child in particular, one is able to develop a love for children. Jesus is "my Lord and my God" at the same time that he is the Savior of all men. As the existential and personal Christ, he liberates. As the universal Christ, he reconciles men with each other. The Savior of each people is Lord of all.

Jesus is our contemporary. It is his life, cross, and resurrection that bring healing and power to our lives. Some challenged Paul's right to apostleship. The right to bear the title of apostle was limited to those leaders who had known Jesus during the days of his flesh. Paul insisted that even though he did not know Jesus in the flesh, he knew him in the spirit. It was Kierkegaard who made us aware of the existential Christ, who is alive in our present experience through faith. The awareness of Christ as living and present in our experience is central to our understanding of Jesus as Lord. Jesus leads us to a new self-understanding. It is as we suffer with him and are rejected with him that we bear the burden of discipleship. It is by participation in his cross that we become aware that grace is costly. We, as black Christians, have always known that grace is expensive. We have borne a cross on each shoulder through "the heat of the day." On one shoulder we have endured "the ills that flesh is heir to." We have known the suffering native to all humans, and especially that of discipleship. But, on the other shoulder we have carried a cross that is the direct result of the injustices, indignities, and inhumanity that whites have inflicted upon blacks in this society. I agree with Malcolm X when he was asked by whites, "What may we do for blacks?" His answer was: "Nothing!" The cross, the task, for whites is not *taming* black power—it is *humanizing* white power. The white Christian's cross-bearing will be in the suburbs and not in the black ghetto.

Jesus, as most whites understand him, "is not enough" for blacks. He solves personal problems for them. Blacks have to deal with sociopsychological problems. A black aide of President Nixon visited a large church body in session in the heart of Alabama. He criticized the blacks severely for hating and killing each other. He took them to task for their shortcomings. But he did not delve into the deep economic, familial, and social roots of black misery that can be traced to white racism. He indicted us for being on our knees, but he did not tell the white oppressor, especially his own "boss," to get off our necks.

This society is seriously ill and white racism is one of its deadly diseases. We cannot simply treat symptoms; we must get to the root causes.

Sandy was a white woman who married Tom, a black man. Sandy had been a stripper and Tom a musician and drug addict. Sandy and Tom were two wonderful people when I met them. Their changed lives were a miracle of grace. Sandy had been born out of wedlock, the child of her mother's interracial affair with a Mexican. Her mother used lemon juice to keep Sandy from turning dark. She took out on the girl her racist feelings and her guilt feelings. Because of the abuse she received as a child, Sandy turned to prostitution. She went as far as she could go. She learned to hate her own people. Sandy and Tom discovered each other in the "hog pens" with the "swine." Their love and conversion experiences have transformed them into a wonderful couple. This true story illustrates the nature of white racism and how it shatters the lives of individuals. And unfortunately for this couple, their hardships may have just begun, because society has not fully accepted their kind of marriage.

No Jesusology based upon salvation one by one will put an end to this social evil. Jesus comes to the black man as Lord of all life, confronting systems of evil that dehumanize the oppressed. To free the slave without destroying the system that enslaves is not to bring a new order into being. Racism is institutionalized as well as personalized in this society. The Jesus who brings personal salvation also brings into being a more humane order. This is the basis for a Christian involvement in bringing a more liberating order into being. Jesus is priest. He consoles the troubled. But he is also prophet. He disturbs those who are at ease

in a racist Zion. Jesus speaks to the humanization of the
social context in which personal decision, action, and life
must take place. The quest for personal peace is not
enough; there must be *social salvation* as well. For blacks
there is no split between personal and social existence; the
two are inseparable. Jesus as the Liberator is also the
Savior. The social and the psychological dimensions of life
and faith must be merged into one whole. Blacks know
of no personal salvation that does not embrace the social
concerns of life. I am not moved to tears when George
Wallace quotes from the Twenty-third Psalm, because I
am more concerned about his social and political program.
The same might be said of Billy Graham, the preacher,
and Richard Nixon, the politician—birds of a feather. This
illustrates the kind of piety we can do without. The Jesus
we understand is one whose piety issues into activism—the
One who leads us from the mountain peak of transfigura-
tion to the valley of decision and action.

For blacks, Jesus is understood in a psychocultural
sense. He leads us to a new self-understanding. He helps
us to overcome the identity crisis triggered by white oppression of blacks. It is related to the affirmation of blackness as the antidote to self-hatred. It is the assertion of our
dignity, our manhood, our peoplehood. Jesus brings a
message from a God who creates, redeems, and judges all
men. In nature and in grace we are sons of God. We are
somebody. We identify with the Jesus of the oppressed,
who enters into life. Jesus who is Emmanuel is the black
Messiah. The "white Christ" alienates us. He symbolizes
the oppressor and intensifies our identity crises. The black
Christ turns us on, so to speak. Jesus as the liberator
confronts us in the symbol of "soul."

Finally, the black Christ liberates and the universal Christ reconciles. The Jesus of the disinherited sets us free. The Jesus who breaks through the color line reconciles all men. But all persons must be confronted by Jesus and take seriously his personal claims on their lives and their people before he can become Lord of all. We cannot fully know Jesus in the role of reconciler until we know him in his role as liberator. The way to a knowledge of Christ as reconciler passes through his "liberator role." *Jesus means freedom!*

6

The Gospel of Power

The gospel is the good news of God. It speaks of the fact that God, by his grace, has forgiven sin and reconciled man with God. The good news is that where there is repentance and faith, there is forgiveness and reconciliation. The gospel is also good news to man in his social relations. Because of a broken relationship between man and God, there is hostility between man and man. Through God's redemptive action in Christ, the wall of participation between men has been removed. This means that the gospel which reconciles us to God also brings us together. Because of man's fall, man being the crown of creation, all creation groans to be redeemed. The good news is that in and through Christ there is a new order of reconciliation between nature, man, and God.

Liberation from liberty is a state of free will or a condition of being free. Freedom from bondage is one important way of expressing what God has done for us through Christ. Jesus came to bring "deliverance to the captives." While liberation and freedom are used interchangeably, *liberation* is the stronger word. Liberation is a radical term.

It implies a shake-up of the *status quo* that benefits only those who are already doing well. It implies the sharing of wealth and power with the disinherited. It means incentives and hope for those lost in generations of despair who ride upon a vicious circle of misery. Liberation implies a new man and a new order. Not only must the oppressed go free, but the order that oppresses must likewise be transformed into an order of liberation.

Liberation is not a proper term for white liberals or black moderates, both of whom desire to have their cake and eat it too. It is not for those who seek peace at any price. It is a proper term only for those who opt for radical changes in the priorities of this social order. The very foundations of the relationship between blacks and whites in this society must be altered, if we are to realize a humane order. The whites-*over*-blacks relationship based upon accommodation for blacks must be shattered. This is the order of oppression, and it is no longer acceptable. We are concerned about the deliverance of a people.

This shake-up of the *status quo* means that liberation must often pass through confrontation. Those who are comfortably situated guard their advantages. Those who are oppressed and would be liberated must keep the pressure on. Confrontation is a manly art. It takes courage as well as common sense to face the powerful if you belong to the powerless. Confrontation is always at the risk of violence. Martin Luther King's life testifies to this. Although he believed totally in nonviolence, his protests always stimulated violence. This was not his purpose, and he was not at fault. It was those who refused to share power and wealth with the black and the poor who responded violently. Whenever the underdog, the black man in this society, refuses to accommodate himself to the paternalism of the white man, conflicts are inevitable. Thus, rejection and suffering and even death itself may be the lot of the oppressed who seek liberation.

The city of Birmingham, Alabama, in the heart of the South as well as of the Bible belt, symbolizes our liberation struggle. Persecution and martyrdom are not strangers to blacks there. It was there that black children were killed in Sunday school during the height of the civil rights movement. Those who worship in the Sixteenth Street Baptist church, those who stay in motels and hotels, and those who eat at integrated lunch counters in Birmingham should remember the supreme sacrifice of those who suffered and died for freedom. It was in Birmingham that police dogs attacked those who marched for freedom. It was there that Dr. King wrote his famous letter on racial justice from his prison cell. His message reminds one of the forceful message of Paul's prison epistles or Bonhoeffer's *Letters and Papers from Prison*. It was in Birmingham that a courageous white pastor split his church over blacks who desired membership in the body of Christ. It was from Birmingham that Angela Davis came, one of the most brilliant and gifted women of our day, a revolutionary in the cause of black liberation. The price of freedom is well known in Birmingham. There are many other places where the struggle for liberation has gone on, violently as well as nonviolently. This says that we are a people determined to be free. Our dignity as human beings is questioned, and this is a matter that must be set straight. We will continue to confront the oppressor as men, and demand our freedom—it belongs to us by natural law, by constitutional right, and by grace.

Black as well as white women are operating out of a new consciousness. But the new consciousness of blacks is not to be mixed or confused with that of white students or women. Whites always have a choice; they can always become "square" and join the mainstream. Our only choice is resistance! resistance! resistance! We have been oppressed consistently from the slave coasts of Africa, through the Middle Passage, through slavery and discrimination to the present. Black history is filled with the oppression and suffering of our people. We bear the mark of oppression in our individual psyches and deep in our collective unconscious. Howard Thurman is correct:

> There is no waking moment or sleeping interval when one may expect respite from the desolation and despair of segregation.

He continues:

> The fact that the first twenty-five years of my life were spent in Florida and Georgia has left its scars deep in my spirit and has rendered me terribly sensitive to the churning abyss separating white from black. Living outside of the region, I am aware of the national span of racial prejudice and the virus of segregation that undermines the vitality of American life.[1]

This awareness of unjust treatment has always been ours. From 1954, with its landmark education decision by the Supreme Court, this situation of injustice has been dramatized. Victories and defeats in the struggle for black liberation have been seen in the headlines and on national television. It was through the ministry of Martin Luther King, Jr., that this awareness was kindled to white heat. But in many ways, as a result of the cry for black power, this awareness has deepened and broadened. So intense has been this new awareness that it has engulfed most black people. Within recent years, through a search for cultural roots independent of the majority culture, most blacks have passed through an identity crisis directly through their own experience or indirectly through their children or grandchildren. We as a people will never be the same and will never relate to the oppressor in the same docile and servile manner. We have affirmed our manhood and our peoplehood. We have laid claim to our humanity. This new consciousness is the basis of our quest for liberation in body as well as in spirit, here as well as hereafter. We now understand that the gospel as gospel is a power for the liberation of the oppressed. We believe that Jesus came to set the captives free.

It has been interesting how much trust is invested in black religion and the black church in spite of its many failures. Sterling Plumpp, a black clinical psychologist, has written on what he calls "black rituals." Plumpp discusses what he calls "faith." He feels that even though he speaks of faith, it turns out to be a robust humanism. Belief gives man a strong purpose, a strong trust in himself "as lord of the physical universe." [2] He rejects black popular belief because it centers its trust in a *white* Christian God. Yet Plumpp's positivistic humanism is the very stuff out of which Euro-American civilization is built. It is not "African" or "black."

Prentiss Taylor, in an essay on "black identity," takes an affirmative attitude toward black religion. He says:

There are very healthy uses for all that fervent energy we have been shunting into weeping and shouting about "dear, sweet Jesus" all these years. Without a doubt, the

Black Church (and the Black Preacher) once performed a very important function as an agency for mass catharsis (to enable us to deal with the virulent white oppression of Slavery time and Freedom/Lynching periods). It is now important to study the thermodynamics of that Faith-force, and to channel it for the benefit of our liberation struggle.[3]

It is the business of black theology to enlighten those who look to the black church for power and for light concerning the nature of that gospel which is the foundation of the black church. There are those who would conveniently use the church for ends that are not inherent in her nature and witness. The real question is whether the gospel of Jesus Christ is like aspirin or like dynamite, whether it is a gospel of pacification or a gospel for revolution, whether it is a gospel of the *status quo* and the Establishment or a power for the liberation of the oppressed. Black theologians agree that it is a gospel which disturbs the consoled, and that its mission is liberation.

In Rom. 1:16, Paul describes the gospel as "the power of God unto salvation." But we ask, What is salvation? Is it spiritual only or does it include the whole man? The reason why white Christians could support slavery, lynching, and all manner of discrimination and still consider themselves devout and heavenward bound was that they had an inadequate understanding of man and salvation. Salvation is for the whole man in community. It affirms our humanity and our cohumanity. Salvation for many whites has been and still is a partial experience. It is at once individual and otherworldly. Insofar as the Jesus movement partakes of this shortcoming, it is a disservice to its adherents and the social mission that white youths had so nobly begun. This split between soul and body, between the sacred and the secular, and between this life and the next has been highly exploited by white racists. Blacks have always known the inconsistency between spiritual freedom and physical bondage. Now we are very aware of the conflict between the socioeconomic deprivation of blacks and false piety and soulless charity.

George D. Kelsey writes concerning the current misunderstanding of social Christianity on the part of Southern Baptists. What they reject, according to Kelsey, is nothing other than the prophetic tradition of Biblical faith.[4] Sam Hill describes Christianity among Southern whites as carrying on until this day the very attitude that was prevalent during the era of slavery. Salvation is personal and not social. It is basically an assurance of a status and a witnessing to that status by telling and calling others to the same kind of confession of faith. It consists of passing out leaflets proclaiming that "Jesus saves." It consists of revivals and a rush in tears to confess sins and accept Jesus Christ as personal Savior.[5] This type of split Christianity takes many forms. It reveals itself sometimes in an enchantment with theological scholasticism and proficiency in Biblical languages minus any social consciousness. It sometimes manifests itself in Pentecostalism that exalts speaking in tongues and spiritual ecstasy but ignores the ethical implications of love, justice, and mercy. Thus in many ways white Christians evade asking the question, "Who is my neighbor?" Furthermore, such people have no understanding of the gospel that recognizes the existence of collective sins, including the institutionalization of racism in this society. Their personal, split gospel does not touch social sin or the real structure of evil.

This misunderstanding of the gospel is nationwide. It is

more than a malady of Southern whites. White liberals often see social sins as real, but they do not give sufficient attention to personal sin and guilt. In their attempt to secularize Christianity, they have lost sight of transcendent realities. They have abandoned the source of power. They have either secularized the holy or sanctified the secular to such an extent that the church has lost its power and is in danger of losing its soul.

Until recently black theologians have repeated the social gospel of white liberal theologians. They were not aware that even the social gospelers did not give adequate attention to racism. Their theology was not informed by black experience and did not speak to the black condition. Martin Luther King, Jr., despaired in his search through the most liberal and socially conscious white theologians. He looked for a theology that could tackle racism on a massive scale. This is what led him outside of Christianity and to Gandhi. He sought and adopted Gandhi's demonstration of love, which had freed a whole people. Other blacks have followed the fundamentalists and have been eaten up with piety and enthusiasm. They repeat the same shibboleths as the whites they admire. These blacks feed on opiate passages of the Bible, especially those which refer to meekness and the afterlife. They give longevity to the magnolia myth of satisfied slaves and docile servants. This position has brought emotional release and inner peace that has made black suffering endurable. But it is a retreat from black reality. What we need is an understanding of the gospel that will not only heal our wounds but also do away with what is hurting us as a people. We need a revolutionary and power-laden version of the gospel.

The significance of the present black theological movement is that for the first time black theologians are doing their own thinking. We are searching the Scriptures and reflecting upon the faith in the light of our heritage, our needs, and our concerns. We have discovered a theology built into our tradition— a soul theology rooted in our Afro-American past. The roots of black theology are found in black spirituals, gospels, and blues, in our poetry and prose, in our art, sermons, and folklore. We have a wealth of spiritual riches that we can feast upon and even share with others who are spiritually barren in a secular culture. No great world religion was born in Europe, and today the heirs of Euro-American culture are searching diligently in the non-Western world for spiritual riches. We blacks are heirs of one of the most spiritually abundant cultures in the world. It is a pity that we were so late in recognizing and cultivating this religious tradition. Those of us who have spent years in theological investigation wonder why we have opted for imitation stones in the white man's theology and church when the white man has left untapped a treasure house of spiritual riches in the black religious experience. This rediscovery of the black man's religious genius came in the late 1960's. At first we were very timid in mentioning it and white scholars easily ruled it out of court. If it were not for the boldness of a James Cone and others like him, the way would not have been opened for exploration into the Afro-American religious tradition.

Black religious experience has never separated the sacred and the secular. Many of our entertainers got their first lesson in "soul" in the choir of a black church. Some have edged their way back to gospel singing after teenagers started singing gospel. The path has been difficult for some who have the jingle but not the music. A depth of quality is found in Mahalia Jackson's music that is missing in some other gospel singers, for she stayed with the black church. By nurture and experience she maintained a depth of commitment and spirituality that gave power and depth to her voice. In the music of Mahalia Jackson, as in Aretha Franklin and some others, we find a close affinity between the sacred and the secular in black experience.

Our independent thinking has enabled us to distinguish between "whiteanity" and Christianity. In the past we were dependent upon white theologians and exegetes. White American scholars relied very heavily upon European scholars, especially Germans, for every word of wisdom, as if they were without thoughts and experiences of their own. There is some indication that white Americans have exhibited an inferiority complex vis-à-vis the Europeans in intellect and culture, while joining all whites in putting down Africans and Asians as the lowest form of human existence. White Americans have translated European theological programs, which are usually concerned mainly with theories and abstract systems of belief, into a theological program that sanctifies the *status quo* vis-à-vis the black and the poor in this country. Theology has served the racial and cultural interests of the white interpreter of European theological programs. It would be dishonest not to allow for the exception. There have, however, been few truly American theological programs.

The preaching of white Christianity in this country, from the sermons preached during the time of slavery down to the White House sermons preached *for* Richard Nixon, has been based upon expediency rather than upon the gospel of liberation. We now know that the path to the universal passes through the particular and that the road to the Celestial City passes through Soulville. The gospel—the power of God unto salvation—saves us alive and saves us whole. From the African forests to these shores and to this day, black religion has been concerned with all of life—social, economic and political, as well as spiritual. A gospel of power must be concerned about City Hall, the White House, the Congress, the courts, about decent housing, fair employment, and quality education, about rats and roaches, "the three R's," I.Q. tests, welfare rights, senior citizens, and dependent children. Unemployment, empty stomachs, crime and imprisonment—all forms of black suffering—are in our purview. We are the victims of an unjust and inhuman order. The gospel of power is directed against the entrenched *status quo* interests of a society of institutionalized racism. It is directed against the collective involvement of white churchgoers, as well as nonbelievers, in America's national sin. The gospel of power is good news, for it is a gospel not of appeasement but of radical involvement in the liberation of the oppressed. It is a gospel of social and political action that will usher in a more human order.

Julius Hobson, a black economist in Washington, D.C., is a thorn in the side of many black churchmen who have either exploited the masses of black people or stood indifferently by while masses of black people have endured gross mistreatment. Hobson, an avowed atheist, knows no sacred cows, so to speak. He is critical of anyone, be he holy man or not, who is not actively involved in acts of liberation for blacks. Hobson, like James Forman of the "Black Manifesto," is a strange prophet. But if black theologians and churchmen do not take their task of black liberation seriously, perhaps God will call others into his service. As one militant put it, it will not be necessary to bomb the black church: the pews will be empty.

Gary Marx has included a chapter on black religion in his book *Protest and Prejudice*.[6] He concludes that religiosity and militancy exist in reverse order: the more religious we are, the less we are militant, and the more militant, the less we are religious. Related to this is the fact that the more educated and/or affluent we become, the less we attend church, and the more we are active or successful in this life, the more "lukewarm" we are toward religion. This is so because we have no theology of our own. Even our religious activists are at best informed by the "social gospel," which is often little more than an American civic religion. They invest too much in man's goodness and ability who live in the world as if God were not. Theirs is a shallow and inadequate creed for a suffering race that knows full well man's inhumanity to man. For centuries we have been victims of the demon of racism —we are a long-suffering people who long for liberation from oppression. We need the "triumph of grace" in our theology. Masses of blacks cannot confront life's adversities without the assurance of divine aid. Tillich spoke of God's acceptance of man even though he was unacceptable. We share the broken relation between God and man which is the human condition. In addition we have to deal with the alienation caused by white racism. We are unacceptable sinners and unmeltable ethnics. We are unacceptable unacceptables. Surely we need to know that God cares and enters with power into our condition. No purely human creed that invests all in "the arm of flesh" can answer the depths of our spiritual needs. We need the assurance of the grace and power of God.

Yet black theology is about *life,* for we are not free. The black man is victimized almost daily in some way to remind him that he is not free. Some of the most shocking reminders come when he is trying to get away from it all on a vacation with his family. Racism haunts him at all times and in all parts of the country. Even if he goes abroad, his fellow American has already been there and transported the virus of white racism. In Europe many former colonial powers have their own form of racism even if the black presence is almost nil. Black theology has to deal with the reality of black life. We seek a full life here and now. We believe that there is a heaven present as well as a heaven future. Our experience of black suffering has too often been an endurance of hell present with a promise of heaven future. Black theology is concerned with the actualization of the future in the present.

Black men, in the words of Unamuno, are "men of flesh and bone." We have learned about life by living. Our understanding of God has always been in providential rather than in syllogistic terms. We have felt God's presence and power deep within our souls. Black theology unites faith and life. For us creation is good. The life we live in the body is sacred. We have this treasure in earthen vessels. The spiritual appears and reflects itself through the temporal. This is the meaning of the incarnation. A white youth stunned some Jesus people at "Explo 72" in Dallas by reminding them that if Jesus were present in the nation's capital, he would identify with the oppressed. He would not preach in the White House but on "U" Street among the blacks or at Dupont Circle among the hippies. Black theology addresses itself to "the slum captivity" of blacks. It is a theology that speaks to the liberation of the oppressed. It is a theology based upon a gospel of power which proclaims deliverance to the captives.

Even our hope in the future life reaches into our present. A man who invests all in this life will most likely live to see his dreams crumble like ashes in his trembling hands. To believe that God rather than death has the last word; to believe that goodness and love are stronger than bitterness and hate; to believe that we will be united with our loved ones beyond death; to believe that goodness has its reward and that evil is punished, is a plus rather than a minus in our earthly struggle for justice. We brought with us from Africa a belief that life continues, that family ties are not ultimately severed by death. This belief was kept alive throughout the long night of black suffering. A people cannot live without hope. As a hopeless people we have majored in hope. It may surprise some to be told that their black fathers were able to transform hope in the future life into meaning in the present life. They were able not only to protest injustice in their time but to inspire hope for a brighter day in the here and now for their children.

We have had all along in black religious experience the raw materials for a political theology. Theologies of hope and liberation emerge from a different set of experiences. In black religious experience we have the basis of a theology of a living hope which has been tempered in the heat of black suffering. Black political theology is based upon an understanding of the gospel of Jesus Christ as the power of God to do far more than we ask or think. It is a theology of meaning, protest, and liberation. It is a theology that merges the secular and the sacred. It is a theology that combines the priestly and the prophetic—pietism and activism. In black theology the future breaks into the present. It provides a gospel of power for the black church to undergird its thought, worship, and life. This gospel of power will enable black Christians to have a better self-understanding, to overcome the identity crisis caused by the black reality in America. It will liberate individual black Christians and black congregations as agents of black liberation.

We shall have more to say later about the black church as a personal, social, and political power center for black people. Martin Luther King, Jr., saw in his ministry the relation between faith and action. Some would like to dismiss Dr. King and his methods as passé. Yet no one demonstrated more completely than he the relation between faith and massive acts of liberation for black people. We hear a lot about the fruits of Nat Turner's rebellion, which sent shock waves throughout white America. But in a purely pragmatic assessment, Dr. King's achievements as a prophet of love were as great, if not greater, than those of the prophet of hate, violence, and death. We must reckon with differences in time and circumstance, but we must take seriously Dr. King's theology of involvement and his movement of black masses and churches in "the stride toward freedom." His understanding of the gospel of power was based upon his assertion of "strength to love."

Martin Luther King's program was centered in black religion and the black church. Those who labored and suffered with him sought spiritual renewal in the worship of God in sermon, song, and prayer. The black church gave guidance, inspiration, and power to the movement. It is often perilous to mental health as well as to physical life to get involved in the black liberation struggle without moral convictions and spiritual power. Without the grace of the gospel to confront adversity, we soon "faint and grow weary." It is by waiting upon the Lord that we renew our strength. We cannot, however, remain on the mountaintop; we must get involved in the struggle in the valley. But our success in the valley is determined by the spiritual and moral power generated on the peak of the mountain of prayer and spiritual reinvigoration. We need an interpretation of our faith that leads from the mountain to the valley. We need a theology that unites worship and service, here and hereafter—one that speaks to the whole man. We may sing in one songfest both "We shall overcome" and "Walk together children, don't get weary; for there is a great camp meeting in the promised land."

I once visited Potter's House in Washington, D.C., together with a former student of mine, a military chaplain. Potter's House is a coffeehouse mission of the Church of the Savior. It is located on Columbia Road, Northwest, in the heart of the Spanish-speaking community. Gordon Cosby, himself a retired military chaplain, welcomed us cordially. My chaplain friend was interested in the coffeehouse ministry to servicemen. At Potter's House we had the opportunity to talk with Cosby about his ministry over coffee and in relaxed circumstances. We were deeply impressed both by the man and the magnitude of his ministry. One thing he said was especially profound. He pointed to those who waited on tables and indicated that they were volunteer Christian workers. They were prepared to talk with the lonely and the despondent who wandered into the coffee shop each evening. They ministered to many races and classes of people. But prior to facing "all sorts and conditions of men," they spent time together in Bible-reading, meditation, prayer, and dialogue. They knew the meaning of the gospel of power. They allowed God to speak to them and thus they were enabled to speak to others. We cannot get the world together if our own lives are shattered and if we do not know the meaning of to-getherness in our own fellowship. A black political theology will help us "get it together" and send us forth with a gospel of power to set the black captives free.

7

Unity
Without Uniformity

An existential and culturally rooted approach to theology cannot escape some assessment of the group life of a people. The group life of Africans received a terrible blow under slavery and the socioeconomic realities of life under white oppression. Michael Novak writes concerning the diverse cultural histories of immigrants who have come to this country since 1865.[1] His analysis does not deal with the fact that slavery had dealt an almost mortal blow to black families before 1865. Novak's observations are focused upon black migration to the industrialized Northern cities. The strong family life of white ethnics as well as Puerto Ricans is said to be their main social strength. Novak also notes that white ethnics had at least two full generations of experience in adapting to urban life before the great migration of blacks from the rural South to the urban North. His observation is essentially correct. Injury to the black family is the cruelest injustice American society administered to blacks. By comparison with other ethnics, he notes:

There is no doubt that Blacks have suffered *more* in America. "Oppression" is a word that has, on the lips of Blacks, at least some meaning and truth.[2]

In Harriet Beecher Stowe's *Uncle Tom's Cabin,* Eliza is the wife of a slave, George Harris. She is the house servant of Mr. and Mrs. Shelby. Shelby sells little Harry, Eliza's son, together with Uncle Tom, to pay debts. The slaves are less valuable than his horses or his wife's jewelry. Eliza is a devout Christian who believes this action to be unjust. She flees with her child to Canada by means of the Underground Railroad. This story attacked the assumption about the happy family life of slaves. Here the family bond is broken. A child is sold from his mother. A wife, in order to escape with her son, has to leave her husband behind. In the story, George Harris runs away and is finally reunited with his wife and son through the help of Quakers. This story is close to the black reality except for the happy ending.[3]

Where there is a structure of evil, there is a need for a gestalt of righteousness. This is a society with white beneficiaries and black victims. The rich get richer and the poor get poorer. Most blacks are poor. Blacks in this society often exist closer to Third World societies than to those who live across town in the South or those who live in the outer city in the North. The one traditional black institution that is powerful enough to oppose entrenched racism in the institutions and the very culture of this society is the black church. Here we speak merely of potential power, power that is mostly underemployed. The hope of black liberation is related to the theology and mis-

sion of this slumbering giant. Both clergy and congregations are now to be aroused as agents of black liberation.

We are concerned about collective sin and guilt, about
social salvation. This does not lessen our concern for personal sins and salvation. The two concerns are interdependent. Most problems that blacks face are set in a social
and cultural context, even if the effect is personal. There
can be no true love of God that does not begin with man.
The church is God's colony in man's world. It has the task
of redeeming all of life as well as the whole of man. For
blacks all problems, whether they be individual or social,
hark back to institutionalized racism.

I was discussing interracial love with a white church
group when the inevitable question of the marriage of a
black man to a white woman came up. My response was
that I would be more concerned about my son than I
would be about the white man's daughter. To put the issue
in bold and broad context, my concern is with black peoplehood. There can be no hope of establishing black
peoplehood without strong black families. Racism has conditioned the black man to see the white woman as the
greatest prize of all, the last social hurdle before his entering the American promised land. But the white woman is
the Trojan horse within the gates of "the black nation."
She is in a position to frustrate the entire cause of black
liberation. The white woman is producing black widows,
orphans, and wrecked homes. Whether prompted by anger
at white men, sexual permissiveness, rebellion against parents, or real love, the white woman is the most effective
destroyer of the development of peoplehood among blacks.
White men possess social, economic, and political power.
The same black males that are able to assert their man-

hood and confront the white power structure are rendered as tame and gentle as babes under the charms and wiles of the white woman. Any would-be leader of blacks at this time must decide. He must not decide for himself and against his people. He must decide for his people and make his personal decisions in the light of his concern for black liberation.

And, most importantly, interracial marriages, whatever the combination, illustrate how racism as a social evil can make personal relationships between blacks and whites extremely difficult, if not impossible. When a white woman marries a black man, the parents lose a daughter; they do not gain a son or grandchildren. The children are half-breeds who are to be absorbed into the black community. The lot of the couple is hard and the burden placed upon their children is often unbearable. The couple may be well adjusted and loving in their courtship and marriage. The rejection comes from the society, which is seriously infected with racism. While marriage is an extremely personal decision, it must exist in a social context. The happiness and well-being of married people has profound social implications. No man is an island, and neither is a couple. When a couple—a white woman and a black man—were introduced on television recently, they noted that the comforts they had were their home, their religion, and each other. The wife stated that she did not let her white friends know that she was married to a black man. Since this was a national television show, one wonders why she was on the show, since some of her white friends were likely to be among the viewers. So serious is this social situation that many interracial couples do not want children. The divorce rate among them is extremely high, and children of these marriages are often extremely bitter toward whites, who have inflicted so much pain upon their parents and upon themselves.

This illustration is not overdrawn; it comes right out of the experience of those who have been greatly hurt by racism. How do we make this society more open so that those who enter into a healthy "colorless" marriage will not be rendered pathological by such great suffering? This is one illustration of the social character of racism. It indicates how individuals are afflicted by this evil even when they seek to go beyond black and white in several meaningful relationships. This applies to our churches. We cannot ignore the institutional nature of racism and really deal with the depths of this sin.

Racism like religion, for many whites, is a personal matter. When I attended a meeting of world religionists, I was approached by a man from a quiet New England town who was quick to confess that he loved all people. He had no black neighbors and was very well off financially. Those blacks he had met were well educated and highly cultured. They were economically comfortable. When he asked me to make a response to his declaration of universal love for all men, I declined. Instead, I urged him to attend my lecture at Harvard Divinity School the following day. It was then that I was to describe the religion and the social and psychological ills of the black poor. It was in this great humanitarian's state and near his home town that my wife and I had been asked to leave a restful vacation cottage years before because the white neighbors were "disturbed by our presence." Such is the nature of white racism in this society. No sentimental confession of undying love for universal man will heal the deep wounds of this society. Declaring that my best friend is a "nigra" or that I know of a superblack man or woman will not liberate the masses of the black victims of racism in this society.

As victims, we know that religion and the institutions through which it expresses itself in the world has to become highly political. Religion and politics have always been "mixed" against the black and the poor in this society. Slogans such as "God and Country," "Law and Order," are commonplace on the lips of devout white churchgoers. But little is said about social justice. The black church, however, cannot ignore the cries of her members who "weep and mourn" for "love, justice, and mercy." We must be informed by and act upon the message of a gospel of power that promises deliverance to the captives.

John Bennett refers to Liston Pope's provocative study *Millhands and Preachers* (1942)—a study made of the churches in Gaston County, North Carolina.[4] On the one hand there were uptown churches catering to the business and professional people. On the other hand there were the mill workers' churches. Religion for the mill workers was an escape from harsh economic conditions. Religion for the business and professional people was a sanction for the *status quo*. Both types of religion were basically perversions of prophetic religion as well as of the gospel of Jesus Christ. This type of separation within the body of Christ has to be overcome if the church is to provide prophetic leadership and an activistic thrust that will break the escapism and overcome the complacency of Christians. Bennett writes:

It is doubtful if any Church can have a very stable hold upon the meaning of the Christian faith unless the members of one class have some contacts with the life of other classes within the fellowship of Christ.[5]

Blacks belong to a subculture within the very structure of American society. Furthermore, the majority of blacks are poor as well. The basis for identity with those bearing "the mark of oppression" already exists. In the words of the apostle Paul, "If one member suffers, all suffer"; this is part of the black reality. We also know what it means to rejoice together in the black community. On the one hand, we know the common sorrow and terror that gripped the helpless black community as it beheld the torture, burning, and dismemberment of a black male whose bullet-riddled body had long since died. On the other hand, we have known common joy as we beheld a Joe Louis whip a white opponent in the ring, or a Jim Brown triumph over his white assailants on the screen by the assertion of his manhood. In all these cases we know the psychological meaning of fellow feeling. Within the fellowship of the black church, the well-off and the down-and-out congregate together, bearing one another's burdens and so fulfilling the law of Christ. Even the well-trained black pastor looks out upon a congregation that represents "all sorts and conditions of men." In his sermon he is required to feed the lambs as well as the sheep. The entire black congregation must include those whom Martin Luther King, Jr., referred to as the Ph.D.'s and the no-D's. "All God's chillun" are present in the black church as they are in the black community. Here we have described a typical black church—not one that has been tampered with by white bodies. When this happens, the black church becomes "uppity," class-conscious, and color-conscious; it becomes a type of social club for the black middle class. In this artificial setting the poor are not welcome, and even if they are present, they are no longer at home.

In his *Ujamaa,* Julius K. Nyerere describes African socialism. According to him, the extended family is the foundation of African socialism. All persons in a tribe are brothers. There is no "enemy list," to use the language of Watergate. Nyerere describes the creed of African socialism as follows: "I believe in Human Brotherhood and the Unity of Africa." [6] The word *ujamaa* means "familyhood." This means that Africans can develop a whole social program out of their traditional heritage by understanding the basic family unit. Nyerere would now update and expand the limits of family life beyond the tribe, even the nation. He speaks, therefore, of a pan-African perspective. In sum he says:

> Our recognition of the family to which we all belong must be extended . . . beyond the tribe, the community, the nation, or even the continent—to embrace the whole society of mankind.[7]

On the positive side of the account, blacks participate in the rich sense of "togetherness" inherited from the African sense of "familyhood." On the negative side of the account, blacks have had to deal with an "extreme situation." This condition has been eloquently described by Rosemary Ruether as follows:

> Today we are witnessing the eruption of a counter-mythology which assaults the foundations of this citadel

of America the Beautiful, declaring that even from the first we had a very parochial view of what it meant to crown our good with brotherhood from sea to shining sea. This counter-mythology arises from the Black community which . . . experienced the underside of the American dream as an American nightmare. For Black men America was always Babylon where they sat down and wept as they remembered their native land. Unlike the Puritan fathers, they did not hasten to these shores voluntarily, filled with dreams of liberty, but were brought in chains packed in the fetid holds of slave ships where only the strong survived.[8]

As perceptive as this statement is, something is missing. It leans too far in the direction of the Black Muslim solution as normative. In this instance black racism is exchanged for white racism. It is a fair exchange, but there is little gain—even for blacks. The black church's total response is far more normative, redemptive, and hopeful. The odd thing is that because we did learn to sing the Lord's song in a strange land, we did not only weep; we rejoiced and laughed as well and have thereby maintained sanity and hope. We are still enduring a situation in which only the strong survive. The black church where the saints still rejoice is not merely a haven of rest; it is also a household of power. What is needed is a theology and a program to move it totally into the push for black liberation. At the moment the black church is not the leader; it is being led. The black church is being propelled by black power and black cultural nationalism while it, within its own right, is the most powerful instrument of black liberation in this society. It need not be unfaithful to the Lord of the church to carry out this mission. It is the mission of the Lord of the church to set the captives free.

Eduard Schweizer observes that Jesus, who called his disciples to follow, still has force. The church has preached a relevant message through all its changing stages of development. It has done so out of a sense of liberty to address itself to burning questions rather than to questions that no longer exist. The Lord accompanies his church through the ages and he is with his disciples now even as he was with those who accompanied him when he walked on earth. Schweizer raises the real question of the contemporaneousness of the church when he notes that what the Palestinian church proclaimed about Jesus and his church was not identical with the message and witness of the Hellenistic church. He then wonders, Is it essential for the Japanese to be converted to a Hebrew, Greek, or European understanding of the gospel? We are assuming in this discussion that Africans and black Americans can reach a deep and redeeming understanding of the nature and mission of the community of faith out of the heritage of the black fathers without ignoring or rejecting the true church—the extension of the incarnation.

John Macmurray is accurate, I believe, as he points to the positive motivation for human community. A community of persons, he observes, as distinct from a society, is a group of individuals united in a common life. Like a society, a community acts together, but unlike a mere society, the members of the community are in communion with one another—they constitute a fellowship.[9] Morally right action is an action that intends community. Community is not merely a group that is functional, cooperating around a particular goal.[10] It is also affective—there is sharing and caring based upon fellow feeling and deep fellowship. *Ujamaa,* "togetherness," "familyhood," is descriptive of community.

Jesus has an elevated place as a social teacher because love was central in his thought and life. The church has failed to make love central in its theology. It has not incorporated love as Jesus viewed it in its creeds and confessions. Belief in God the Father became belief in the first and unbegotten Person of a metaphysical Trinity. Belief in his love has been replaced by an appeal to God's mercy in the name of Christ, who died for sinners. The belief in the triumph of a Kingdom of love and righteousness has been replaced by expectation of joy in heaven and torture in hell.[11]

Love as Jesus understood it is an urge for social cooperation in which the cooperating parties treat each other as persons. The welfare of the individual is furthered by the cooperation of all those who are members of the group. In order for an individual to be personal, he must act from within some group. Individuals are persons in society.[12] The church as a fellowship should provide the climate for the flowering of that which is most truly personal as well as the manifestation of genuine community.

In I Cor., ch. 12, Paul illustrates the nature of the body of Christ by referring to the human body. The human organism presents a unity with a variety of parts. All these parts are organically related and vitally associated with the whole; all in various ways serve one another. The numerous parts of the body are indissolubly related to one another and are of service to one another. Those parts of the body which are accorded a lesser status are indispensable. Those members who are less well endowed do count.

Those who are gifted often attempt to lord it over the humble. In overestimating their powers of authority and leadership, many demonstrate their unfitness for true leadership. Jesus described himself as servant of all and this should be the mark of his followers as well. Every part of the body is vital to the smooth and effective working of the human organism. What is true of the human body is true of the body of Christ, the church.

There is a strong sense of *jen,* "fellow feeling," among the Chinese. It is referred to as "human-heartedness." In the church, the community of faith, there should be a similar compassion one for another. Paul puts it this way: "If one member suffers, all suffer together; if one member is honored, all rejoice together" (I Cor. 12:26). If we have a headache, the entire body is out of order. If we suffer a foot injury, our consciousness is full of pain. Sickness and health concern the entire organism. In the Christian community we are to suffer and rejoice together. As it is written in another New Testament epistle, Christians are to "bear one another's burdens, and so fulfil the law of Christ" (Gal. 6:2).

Even though there is this unity, every organ of the body has its own function. No organ does the work of another. There are likewise diversities of gifts and functions in the church. Apostles have the duty of transmitting the traditions of the faith. Prophets have the task of revealing the deeper meanings of the traditions as they apply to the life and programs of a given age. Teachers are to instruct in the faith and safeguard sound doctrine from heresy. There are healers, helpers, administrators, and evangelists. Each role is important for the witness of the church in the world.

Every true church in every age should recognize the simple truth that in order for the church to be vital and effective a variety of functions is required. There is to be respect for all persons and all gifts. All are essential and necessary to each other. All are inspired by the same Spirit.[13]

In I Cor., ch. 12, *sōma* ("body") is used in some sixteen verses (vs. 12–27). Chapters 12 to 14 of this epistle are a unit. The interpretation of any one sentence must be congenial to the whole unit. Paul was grappling with a single situation in the life of the church in Corinth.

Paul Minear observes:

> That community was being demoralized by the profusion of spiritual gifts, a profusion that was most apparent when the church gathered for worship. . . . Thus was produced a bedlam of sound and a competitive spirit that was destroying the fabric of fellowship. All this was rationalized and justified by an appeal to the Holy Spirit.[14]

In Paul's mind the issue resolved itself into a matter of understanding the full correlation between the oneness of the Holy Spirit, as the source of gifts, and the oneness of the church, as the area where the gifts were apportioned individually. In I Cor. 12:1–3, Paul associates the Spirit of God with the confession that Jesus is Lord. No spiritual gift comes from God which does not relate to the confession of the Lordship of Jesus Christ. And this confession is sustained by the Spirit. The same God, the same Lord, and the same Spirit are actively present in all bona fide spiritual gifts. No spiritual expression that was not in the service of all and empowered by all was authentic. Every spiritual gift must have a oneness in source and goal, a oneness that was itself manifested by the variety in the gifts themselves. Unity was not uniformity. It was not the source of uniformity and was not served by it. It is clear that there were to be varieties of gifts, but the same Spirit. Every gift was to be used for the common good. For example, emphasis was not to be placed upon a particular prophet, but rather upon the work of the Spirit through prophecy.[15]

> All gifts and services must be regarded as essential to the one body. . . . Pluriformity of gifts, services, and achievements was necessary; exclusive claims for any one of them were impossible. Thus discord among the recipients of the various gifts was ruled out by their interdependence in the Spirit, in the Lord, and in God. No recipient who was proficient and energetic in the use of any *charisma* could appeal to the superiority of his gift over that of others.[16]

Paul desired to restore the sense of interdependence among believers. This required a true sense of their mutual relation to Christ. "One body" implies a common good. It means absolute solidarity in suffering and glory. The image of the body expressed the reality of the unity and the plurality to the service of Jesus, the work of God, and the gift of the Spirit.

The edification of the church was to be the test of all gifts (I Cor. 14:3–5). This replaced self-glorification. All was for the building up of the church. To discern the body of Christ in worship is to observe the gifts being used in the service of community. Those who have been baptized by the Spirit into one body (I Cor. 12:13) must be moved by a sense of fellow feeling for the common good.

Love is the "more excellent way." Love is that which makes every other gift valid. Divorced from love, all other gifts are useless. Love belongs to the Kingdom that never ends. Love can never be obsolete. Thus it outstrips prophecy, even martyrdom. Love defines the meaning of *sōma,* or "body." It produces the varieties of gifts and unifies them in the service of others—the world and God as well. Love sums up what Paul meant by "varieties of gifts, but the same Spirit; . . . varieties of service, but the same Lord; . . . varieties of working, but . . . the same God" (I Cor. 12:4–6). I Corinthians, ch. 12, has major ecclesiological importance.

> The gift and service of love was the manifestation of the pluriform unity of the members in the one body. The image of the body and the image of love should for all significant purposes be considered one image; they cannot, in fact, be considered otherwise, since the primary content of both is determined by the image of Christ.[17]

The black church is not one uniform structure. It is a good example of what Minear has called "pluriformity." It is a unity-in-diversity. Many of the deep concerns of black churches transcend denominations and creeds. There is at present a "black ecumenism." It is represented in the National Committee of Black Churchmen, but it embraces Catholics as well as Protestants, Jews and Moslems as well as Christians, and it even includes "nonbelievers" in a traditional sense within the black community. There is, therefore, unity without uniformity among blacks, and this is manifest in black churches in a particular way.

There are those like William L. Banks who take an evangelical perspective of the Billy Graham type. The church is a loose federation of "saved" individuals. Banks renounces the "institutional" type of church that has adopted the ideas and programs of the social gospel.

> The ideal social gospeler is the preacher who seeks to establish an institutional type church, stresses the here and now, engages in politics, fights for civil rights, and believes in black power, black reparations, and black theology. . . . He lays claim to the acts of Old Testament prophets. However, the prophets' social teachings and Christ's physical healing ministry are not criteria for determining the church's role in society.[18]

Banks views as the corrective for this social Christianity a proper understanding of the church in the Epistles, which, as he understands them, portray a dispensational view of history. One must distinguish between the New Testament church and the nation-state of Israel. The Old Testament prophets were under law; the New Testament church is under grace. Christ was somewhat concerned about the poor, but the main task of the church is to win individuals to the Christ of Calvary.[19] According to Banks, the social gospel is a manner of "flirting with the world." [20]

We could ignore Banks if his version of Christianity were an isolated phenomenon among blacks. Unfortunately, it is widespread. Black theology is not identical with the social gospel. The social gospel was informed by the Euro-American experience. It was concerned mainly with social and economic problems of whites. It did not hit racism head on. It was extremely optimistic about man. Banks is not able to sort these things out. His views recall the Christianity of the era of slavery and of the quietistic fundamentalists who place all their trust in personal evangelism and heavenly rewards. He echoes Billy

Graham's assertion when he says that he is a New Testament evangelist and not an Old Testament prophet. He does not share the conviction of Martin Luther King, Jr., that the God of Amos is the God of Jesus.

Banks writes:

> All attempts to improve society will fail unless the hearts of men are changed. Boycotts or selective patronage, sit-ins, picketing and mass demonstrations are all carnal weapons of the world, calculated to achieve certain carnal, external, materialistic ends, but which have no beneficial effect upon the heart. All action by Christians which is unconcerned about man's soul, unconcerned whether he accepts the shed blood of Christ, of necessity is an action which belongs to this world system, a system which is evil.[21]

This is a gospel for the *status quo,* one that no longer has currency. It is part of the gospel, but it is not the *whole* gospel, and it cannot liberate the complete person. It can do nothing toward the liberation of a people, and this is what the black struggle is all about. Does Banks see all black ministers who oppose his view as Rev. Ike's? Rev. Ike has the view that money is "the root of all good," and that the Christian goal is "pie in the sweet bye and bye NOW!" As a multimillionaire, Rev. Ike is skimming the cream from the top. His followers are often very poor and so they live vicariously through him. As one admirer of Adam Clayton Powell, Jr., once said of him, "The cat is *living!*" Fortunately, the view of Banks regarding what I am calling a political understanding of the gospel is not the only one even among black evangelicals. Tom Skinner is constantly pushing evangelicals toward a gospel of total liberation of blacks—in body as well as in spirit. James Forbes is a pentecostal who is making the same point.

Albert Cleage has a field day when he encounters this anti-institutional type of black religion. He has been affectionately referred to as "the prophet of the black nation." He does stand in direct lineage to Marcus Garvey, "the black Moses." Cleage opposes "piety religion" and considers churches under pietistic leadership as "comfort stations." He will have none of that kind of religion which only satisfies individual souls and guarantees individual salvation. Cleage has some understanding of this type of religion in spite of his taking exception to it. This religion has offered a very necessary psychological relief for an oppressed people. It enabled us to maintain our sanity. It provided escape from brutality and oppression. Once a week we went to church and received the strength to endure another week. We delighted in contemplating life after death. This was one means of escape "from the troubles of this world."

This sort of religion was perhaps the only escape for the "Sunday morning" blacks. The "Saturday night" crowd had sex and alcohol, and of course drugs. Some black churchgoers enjoy the best of both worlds. Cleage does not indicate the positive value of worship and its relation to the prophetic as well as the priestly ministry of the church. Protest as well as meaning relates to the whole person and all of life. Cleage is obsessed with the black nation, the collective black man. He does not give proper attention to the need to make individuals healthy and whole in order that they may fulfill their life and purpose within the black community. Cleage's view is thus stated in creedal form:

> I believe that both my survival and my salvation depend upon my willingness to reject individualism and so commit my life to the Liberation Struggle of Black people and ac-

cept the values, ethics, morals, and program of the Black Nation defined by that struggle, and taught by the Black Christian Nationalist Movement.[22]

Cleage also observes:

As Black Christian Nationalists we understand power and human nature. . . . We are oppressed by a group whose power depends on its ability to maintain its cohesion. . . . The oppressed tend to come together because they have no alternative. Either they come together or they die. So gradually Black people are being driven together, just as white people are being driven apart.[23]

It is sad indeed if blacks are driven together only by their common misery—or merely because "misery loves company." This is not the stuff out of which community is developed. Real togetherness needs deep caring and purpose. Surely religious experience and the whole history of the black church provides a sounder basis for community than this.

Banks overstates his case for black quietism, piety, and individualism. Cleage does the same for black nationalism and the black collective consciousness. Both emphasize half-truths and only part of the perspective we need to build true community. What we need, however, is a balance between the emphasis on the whole man as a person and the emphasis on a healthy life in community. Blackness does present a real group challenge. It is a personal challenge. It is a challenge in respect to ourselves and our total experience. We have seen in this discussion that a strong black community can only exist through strong black families and that the strength of black families touches upon our most intimate personal relations in sex and marriage.

We must be part of a communal effort to define and control our experience. There is a community among us between the dead, the living, and the unborn. Jews are aware of this sense of community. This is the reason why rabbis are applying sanctions against those in their midst who officiate at "mixed" marriages between Jews and non-Jews. Our threat comes from interracial love and marriage between white women and black men. We cannot, as we have seen, build a strong family system upon which the black community depends without black males' being willing to resist the temptations and even pleasures of consorting with white women, who, after all, belong to the oppressing community. More blacks and whites are sleeping together, but as far as the masses of black people are concerned, conditions are not getting any better. The black community has a prior claim upon our time, our talents, and our resources. The challenge to build "familyhood" centers in the strengths of black families and the black church.[24]

This sense of *ujamaa,* "togetherness," was eloquently expressed in an open letter from James Baldwin to Angela Davis when she was in a California prison. Baldwin wrote:

> If we know, then we must fight for your life as though it were our own—which it is—and render impassable with our bodies the corridor to the gas chamber. For, if they take you in the morning, they will be coming for us that night.[25]

Leon Sullivan illustrates what may be described as a new church-style for black Christians. Sullivan, a black pastor and head of Opportunities Industrialization Centers (OIC), sees the church as a household of power. For him, the church is more than a voice; it is a demonstration of

God for men on earth. Sullivan is convinced that the basic solution to the problems of our society must come by the efforts of the church, because the church is God's agent working toward the ultimate solution of all human problems. He believes that "God loves and helps the underprivileged." Sullivan's sense of mission, his ministry, is in black economic development. Taking the social proclamation of Jesus to the home folk at Nazareth (Luke 4:18–19) with all seriousness, he declares that one cannot bring salvation to a child whose stomach is empty, whose feet are bare, and whose body is naked. Heaven is coming, but until that day, the pearly gates can take care of themselves. He goes on to sum up his sense of mission as follows:

> I saw the need for the Samaritan of our time who would stop and reach down and take off his clothes, if necessary, to wrap the wounds of a bleeding brother. I was challenged to participate in a ministry that was not only of the pulpit, but was of the streets, an enacting, living, lifting, pulsating, saving ministry. . . . I was convinced that a man's body and soul could not be separated. . . . The ultimates of eternity are intertwined with man's physical person and his spiritual person.[26]

When I was in Japan, it was my privilege to look at a number of the new religions. The Soka Gakkai, or Value Creating Society, is one of the largest and most progressive among these postwar religious movements. Like most of the "new religions," this movement is a mixture of several traditional religions and sects. It is obvious that among other things the "family system" of Confucianism has greatly influenced this movement. Conversion efforts are aimed at whole families. It is believed that when a mother is enlisted as a member, she will win the entire family to the movement. A family membership is assumed and anticipated when there is a conversion of any member. In a similar manner a Jewish rabbi may reckon his membership in terms of families. This is in essence the model which the new black church-style must follow. While we will take our cue from the practice of "familyhood" rooted in our African heritage, it will provide in the black church that reality of community which will make of it at once a family of God and a household of power.

8

Ethics and Eschatology

The question of black hope in relation to black suffering is so crucial that a black political theology should give some attention to it. The future of black religion and the black church may well depend upon what black theologians can contribute to a correlation between eschatology and ethics in the black experience. The charge of otherworldliness is incessantly brought against the black church by black youth. Many youths would be promising leaders of the black church and work through it for the cause of social justice if they could be assured that black religion, including the theology that moves the black church, *really cares* about the plight of the black poor *here* and *now*.

Christians are to consider seriously the eschatological outlook of Jesus and what this means for ethics. Another way of stating the case would be to consider the ethics of the Kingdom in relation to the mission of Jesus. We might also examine the relationship between the ethics of the Jesus of the Gospels and the earliest Christian community. To deal with any of these questions is a real challenge to scholarship. Amos Wilder's statement of the case is essentially correct:

> The task of stating what the original teaching of Jesus Himself was, either as regards eschatology or ethics . . . is one beset with immense obstacles. Scholarship is ever more aware of the difficulty of drawing a line between the *ipsissima verba* and the sayings ascribed to Jesus in the gospels but bearing the stamp of later formulation. The Jesus of the synoptic gospels, even the Jesus of our oldest sources, is a figure whose outline has already been modified unconsciously in the thinking of the church. In any case an effort must be made and has been made with good results to distinguish some of the clearer modifications which the tradition has undergone, by the use of criteria open to us. On the basis of these, a working hypothesis as to the historical Jesus and His teaching can be presented.[1]

Both ethics and eschatology are essential to black political theology. They are interdependent and inseparable. One cannot see the present life in full focus without a look at the future life, but neither may one fully appreciate the future life apart from the present life. When life is seen as a unity and man is understood in his wholeness, even death becomes an experience within life.

Eschatology can no longer be a mere addendum to black theology. It is at the center of any theology which endeavors to bring a meaningful hope to the weak and the powerless. Ethics is also pivotal to a theology that is concerned with the liberation of the oppressed in the here and now. Black theology has a unique promise of ushering eternity into time without surrendering a grasp upon eternal hope. What we seek is not *quantity* of existence but *quality*. James Cone writes:

> No eschatological perspective is sufficient which does not challenge the present order. If contemplation about the future distorts the present reality of injustice and reconciles the oppressed to unjust treatment committed against them, then it is unchristian and thus has nothing whatsoever to do with him who came to liberate us.[2]

Reacting to Bultmann and affirming Moltmann, Cone sums up his position on eschatology as follows:

> Hope must be related to the present, and it must serve as a means of transforming an oppressed community into a liberated—and liberating—community. Black Theology does not scorn Christian hope; it affirms it. It believes that, when people really believe in the resurrection of Christ and take seriously the promise revealed through him, they cannot be satisfied with the present world as it is. The past reality of the resurrection and the future of God disclosed through it makes persons restless with the imperfections of the present. . . . Christians must fight against evil, for not to fight, not to do everything they can for the brother's pain, is to deny the resurrection.[3]

Cone points out that slave masters emphasized heaven in order to transfer the focus of slaves' loyalties away from present reality and toward life after death. The rise of black theology and black power has now changed this focus. Blacks now believe something can be done about this world. Heaven no longer means accepting injustice in this world while staking all upon life over yonder.[4] We have had our fill of pearly gates, golden streets, and long white robes. We have sung songs about heaven until we are hoarse, but our poverty and misery have gone unabated.[5]

Cone is correct when he asserts that we do not need to reject life after death because whites have distorted the hope grounded in Christ's resurrection for selfish ends. We must redefine eschatology in view of the liberation quest.

> If God is truly the God of and for the oppressed for the purpose of their liberation, then the future must mean that our fight for freedom has not been for naught. Our movement in the world cannot be a meaningless thrust toward an unrealizable future, but a certainty grounded in the past and present reality of God.[6]

So far so good! Up to this point, I find myself saying "Amen" to the manner in which Cone has skillfully related eschatology to ethics. But now he takes what I consider a suicidal course rather than an empirical and sane approach to the present situation. Instead of indicating concrete ways in which eschatology can give drive and direction to liberating programs for the oppressed, he tells us that those "who die for freedom have not died in vain; they will see the Kingdom of God." [7] In spite of the firepower of the oppressors, we are urged to risk all; for "it does not matter that white people have all the guns and that, militarily speaking, we have no chance of winning." [8] We are told that "we do not have to worry about death if we know that it has been conquered and that as an enemy it has no efficacy. Christ's death and resurrection have set us free." [9]

One wonders if Cone really believes what he says here. Is it the only conclusion he can reach that is consistent with the rather Barthian slant of his entire program? Is it

said for the shock treatment he desires to give white
churchgoers at ease in Zion? The real danger associated
with the reckless and despairing note sounded by Cone is
that it could be like a boomerang turning in upon black
youth themselves. The incidence of blacks killing blacks
and taking their own lives is too great for us to tolerate an
eschatological position that sanctifies despair and encour-
ages the use of a type of "teleological suspension of the
ethical" in the name of theology. Surely black theologians
must be responsible, especially at this time, when they are
being widely read by angry youths who are not capable of
ethical, metaphysical, and theological points of distinction.
We have the task, even the burden, of rendering in clear,
concise, and concrete terms how the Christian faith may
implement black power here and now in constructive programs for the liberation of the oppressed. Feeding the fa-
naticism of the masses is not worthy of so noble a task.
And thus, while Cone has given a greater weight to eschatology in this work than in his first volume, he leaves
much to be desired in his ethical program.

We are told that the future breaks into the present, but
we must be willing to give up our lives in the present with
the assurance that we have a future in the Kingdom of
God. Only blacks who hover on the brink of utter despair
will buy this. We need a bringing together of ethics with
eschatology in a way that will empower blacks for a better
life now. To this end Christians must become colaborers
with God and each other. We must then begin to spell
out what are the theological perspectives on a new self-
image, social solidarity, self-determination, community
control and empowerment programs as well as the message

and mission of the black church in the cause of black liberation. Only in this sense may ethics and eschatology be brought together in black theology. Black people are concerned about "winning" and they are not willing to accept a theology of despair. What they need most is a theology which lifts up God's promises and man's hope. We are a hopeless people who have majored in hope. If we have a mission as black theologians to our people, it is to provide a theological understanding of this hope. It is to indicate how God is at work in the world and how we may join him in the liberation of the oppressed.

It is true that we cannot give ourselves fully to any worthwhile cause until we have conquered the fear of death. Martin Luther King, Jr., was correct when he insisted that one cannot truly live until he has laid hold of something more precious than the present life. There is a sense in which life must receive its ultimate direction from beyond physical death if our life is to be rich and full and if our interest in life is more than longevity and sheer physical pleasure. If all our hope is invested in the pleasures of this life and in its length, we cannot really give ourselves to anything which transcends our sense experience. Only those things within the purview of our senses can claim our attention. *Liberation,* we are told by James Cone, is something that transcends mere preservation of life. "Liberty or death" should be our creed and we should willingly lay down our lives for the freedom of those to follow. It is important that we die as men and not as fools, however. It is important that we die in hope and not out of sheer frustration and despair. A part of our responsibility as mature Christians is to program hope

here and now so that we might experience a measure of
deliverance from oppression for ourselves as well as for
our children.

By uniting ethics and eschatology we are seeking to
take full advantage of the riches that flow into the present
life from an eternal hope without forsaking every constructive means of mapping a program of hope. Eternity
breaks into time when eternal hope and earthly planning
are joined. When ethics and eschatology meet, we can be
led in either of two directions. We may be led either to
withdrawal or to engagement in reference to this life. We
will either resign ourselves to our oppressed condition, seeing it as an unavoidable *fate,* or we will protest our oppressed condition and claim liberation, seeing that as the
proper *destiny* of sons of God. We will become pietistic
in an otherworldly sense or revolutionary in a this-worldly
sense. The gospel will either become salve or surgery, aspirin or dynamite in reference to the established order.
But a black theology must maintain a balance between the
here and the hereafter, between religious celebration and
political action, for it must assert the wholeness of man
and the unity of life. Even death is an experience within
a larger view of life.

The genius of black religion is evident in the way blacks
have been able to juxtapose sorrow and joy, tears and
laughter. Note the contrasting mood in the line "Nobody
knows the trouble I've seen, Glory halleujah!" We have
experienced the American myth as a nightmare because of
white oppression. America is an experience of Babylonian
captivity for blacks, but we have not only been able to sing
the Lord's song in America; we have also been able to
laugh, rejoice, and celebrate. We have been able to praise

God in church and to march in the streets for justice. Jesusology for blacks is not divorced from the quest for freedom and justice in the present life. Religious celebration has given us drive in the push for civil and human life for the black and the poor. Revival and survival are brought together in our understanding of faith and ethics.

We are in need of a deeper understanding of the doctrine of the resurrection. The resurrection rightly understood has meaning for the present life as well as our future hope. The resurrection is the belief held up in our faith which symbolizes ultimate victory over sin, evil, and death. It indicates that God has the last word. The resurrection faith unites creation, redemption, and judgment. The God of the resurrection is our present Lord as well as our future Judge. He is the One who has made us. He is "the maker of heaven and earth." He is benevolent, provident, and gracious. All creation, all history, and all life are within the scope of his Lordship. The resurrection faith has a great deal to do with our attitude toward life, the measure of our concern and the direction of our hope. The God of the resurrection is Lord of life as well as Lord over death. To share in this resurrection experience is to develop a new life-style. If we are raised with Christ, we will seek those things which are above. To believe in the resurrection is to pass through suffering and gross disappointment to victory. This faith assures us that love is stronger than any foe, even death, the "last enemy." It makes all the difference for our lives to know that nothing can estrange us from the love of God.

As people of African descent, we are not strangers to a belief in the communion of saints. For a long period of time we have had a deep reverence for our departed loved ones.

The elders are greatly respected in Africa because they are so close to those loved ones who, having departed this life, are now in the spirit world. But we are told that these ancestors have no lasting spiritual destiny. They belong to the "living dead" as long as someone "living" remembers them. Even their "collective immortality" passes away when the living no longer remember these departed ones. It is because we are heirs of the faith in Christ's resurrection that we will not find fulfillment in this type of eschatology.

We are schooled in a different concept of time. The full range of history includes past, present, and future. Africans, we are told, have only a concept of the past, the present, and a short future. Ernst Bloch is typically Western when he describes man as the *hoper*. Hope requires a strong emphasis upon the future. Belief in progress, which has provided the presuppositions of science and technology in the West, is akin to the theological perspective on hope. Man has to believe that things can be otherwise if he is to involve himself in changing things. It is true of the scientist as it is for the politician. There is to be teleology in hope. We take the responsibility to map the future of hope. So much of the black struggle for liberation has been and remains as hope against hope. We have had so little evidence of change toward the humanization of life and yet we have dared to hope and have inspired hope in our children, who have often become a "living hope," realizing in their lives what their parents could only dream. It follows that black theology emerges out of a tradition in which hope has been kept alive through faith.

As we look at our African past and our Afro-American past and present, we need to work through all the streams of thought and faith which converge in our understanding of ethics and eschatology. It is important that we take the best from our heritage to enrich our understanding of human destiny here and hereafter, personal and collective. How we handle our personal identity crisis as well as our quest for peoplehood is bound up with the relation between ethics and eschatology. All that we are and all that we hope to be as persons and as a people is at stake.

The African contribution to socialism or to peoplehood is precious to us. We need to recover a sense of "familyhood" in our churches and communities. Reverence for ancestors among African people is clearly bound up with the understanding of the common life. What happens beyond death is not separated from social relations here and now. All of life is a unity and death is an experience within life. Thus ethics and eschatology come together in a way that brings enrichment and fulfillment to the present from the vantage point of a frame of reference beyond this life, including a fellowship between the living and the living dead. It would appear that a good case for "baptizing" all this into the Christian faith could be made until we consider the serious differences in the understanding of time just mentioned. Here we have relied very heavily upon John Mbiti's interpretation. All this sounds very much like the "cloud of witnesses" or "the communion of saints" often mentioned in Christian circles. There is both similarity and difference in concepts. This means that careful attention must be paid to our interpretation. What we have in African eschatology appears at times to be "like footprints on the sands of time," giving a new wind to those who survive. Even "social immortality" is less than personal in a conscious sense. If I understand James Cone correctly, he would appear to be close to accepting the offering up of one's life for black liberation as a means toward partaking of a type of social immortality. There is lack of evidence that Cone takes the African roots of black religion with adequate seriousness. Even his quest through *The Spirituals and the Blues* has not radically altered the Teutonic character of his theological insights. We all, including the present writer, must seek to be open more and more to the indigenizing process.

What is precious in the Christian faith is the assurance of a conscious and personal destiny. Personality embraces the whole of life and it is not destroyed by physical death. Man does not lose his "thouness" or his authentic selfhood with physical death. We are assured rather that the self enters into a larger and fuller life as it draws toward a deeper relation with the Lord of life and the Lord over death. As the purpose in human life merges deeper into the divine purpose, life becomes mature and full and partakes of greater knowledge and holiness. Because of the Christian's resurrection faith, there is a new urgency about being and doing the truth in this world and for others. Life is a unity; it is whole and it is sacred. "To be with the Lord" is the highest good for the Christian, whether he lives or dies.

At this time of despair in the experience of many sincere Christians, it is important to clarify the relation between ethics and eschatology in the Christian faith as understood by black Christians. We have always considered Jesus as a divine friend, but Jesusology does not mean that we have given up on social justice in this life. We can shout on Sunday and march for a better welfare program on Monday. Both are part of the Lord's work.

Jesusology for whites means that they have given up on working for change in this world. It means a fundamentalist and individualistic quest for salvation and a withdrawal from social and political involvement. For blacks to believe in Jesus means that they know him as prophet and king as well as priest. The Kingdom is present where the will of God is done, and this can happen now. Life is whole and the future of God breaks into the present struggle for liberation. A liberating experience of reconciliation implies that there can be no ethics without eschatology and no eschatology without ethics. Death is an experience within life, and eternal life is the new life we experience through a saving relationship we have with God, which continues world without end. Eternal life means that we are agents of liberation and reconciliation in the world and among men because we share in the love, justice, and power of God.

9

Black Theology
as Power

Political theology, as a theology, enrolls itself in the attempt to impart the *kerygma* by means of involvement in the human quest for liberation. It is not primarily involved in a repetition of its creeds and dogmas. The situation of man in the world is normative for political theology, of which black theology is an expression. Political theology brings an essential corrective to existential theology because it perceives existence no longer as purely spiritual, but as sociopolitically conditioned.

This approach to theology involves the merger of theory and praxis. It places in the foreground the relations between theory and praxis, religion and society. This praxis, concerned about the liberating transformation of man in the actual sociopolitical arena, is the point of departure in the understanding of faith.[1]

Black religious thought has had a healthy tension between the existential and the ethical. We have been concerned about the meaning of selfhood and personal destiny. The search for meaning has been a constant preoccupation of black writers—nontheological as well as theological. But we have always associated the social context of experience with existential concerns. Because of racism we have had to see the personal problems of black life in the setting of social oppression from which we would be liberated. This has inextricably linked the ethical questions of our existence with the existential. Whereas others may be accepted socially and feel empty in a personal sense, blacks must see social oppression as precipitating a host of personal crises. This is one reason why Eastern religions that are meditative and consoling to the individual in the vein of Peale's "pills" appeal to affluent whites. Islam, a religion with a social and political program, is often more appealing to blacks. Islam speaks of nation-building—of the whole man in community.

The otherworldly religious perspective is no doubt the very essence of sermons preached in the White House to a congregation of persons high up in government with a stake in things as they are. But Watergate reminds us that few sermons are preached in the White House about graft, corruption, and the plethora of social and personal sins. The insensitivity of the powers that be to human misery caused by war, greed, and racism made blacks aware long ago that something was wrong with piety on the Potomac. We knew this long before the price of beef went up or gasoline became scarce. It did not take the revelations of self-righteousness and the callousness reflected in the scandal that has rocked the nation to bring the message of "I don't care about the underdog" home to the black poor. Some who have invested much in the American myth are now seeing the fallacy of that myth as they behold men of great power and privilege acting as if they were above the law and declaring, "Evil, be thou good."

Sherwood Eddy describes three dominant philosophies in American history. First, there was the effort to build a new world in America under the spiritual ideal of the Kingdom of God. Second, there was a secular ideal that later came to be called "the American Dream," based upon democracy "with liberty and justice for all." This ideal was embodied in the Declaration of Independence. And third, there was the factor of selfish individualism, often compounded into mass materialism, tending to pervert or destroy these ideals. Our history has been a checkered one of the interplay of these three forces.

> The American pictured a life that should be better and richer and fuller for every man, and a society providing opportunity for each according to his ability and achievement. . . . The practical and prosperous American, however, was always tempted to yield to materialistic and money standards of value, inspired by sentiments and fictions of pre-established harmony, evolutionary optimism, automatic progress, and Manifest Destiny. He covered the most sordid debasement of ideals by these fictions.[2]

While this characterizes the outlook of the rich and the powerful both in and out of the church, the black poor are to be content with a kingdom not of this world. They are to lick their wounds and be sustained by a gospel of suffering, often written for them by representatives of the oppressing group. The kingdom of love and brotherhood of which Martin Luther King, Jr., spoke is as elusive as ever; it is a mirage in the desert. We are expected to be content with a spiritual kingdom within, to live in a hell in the present, and to eat crumbs from the tables of the rich and the powerful while longing for the glories of heaven. All the talk of the Kingdom from Jonathan Ed-

wards to Billy Graham and from Thomas Jefferson to
Richard Nixon has had nothing to do with those "beyond
the melting pot." The secular ideals of liberty, justice, security, and brotherhood, the very components of the so-
called American Dream, have not been realized in the experience of the oppressed.

Harvey Cox hits the target on dead center when he observes the religious situation in the 1970's and notes the
decline of middle-class denominations. God is seen, however, to be alive and well among conservative churches and
among an increasing number of spiritual sects. Cox is
properly disturbed that what he calls a "Third Great
Awakening" is becoming almost indifferent to "social action." He raises several searching questions that make a
strong case for a political theology: [3]

> Why the emphasis on private values and intimate com-
> munity just when America's imperial arrogance has reached
> its peak? Why the retreat from political theology at just the
> moment when the most "political" President in our history
> is usurping privileges previously exercised by other
> branches and levels of government? Why the apparent sur-
> render of the clear biblical imperatives on war and bigotry
> just as the largest military budget in history robs the needy
> and our Government abandons any effort to assure jobs or
> justice to Black Americans? [4]

The Cox who moved gleefully from "the secular city" to
"the feast of fools" embracing "holy hippies" almost as the
very chosen of God now ponders the meaning of this new
retreat from social evils. He seeks to understand com-
munes, the outpouring of the Spirit, Zen, and transcenden-
tal meditation among modes of current religious expression. He warns:

If any of these should insulate us from the bewildering macro-structural issues of our day, then Jesus' stern words to the whited sepulchres of His day begin to refer to us also.[5]

At this point the black man is tempted to say to Harvey Cox, "Amen! Brother!"

Roger Shinn has made an important contribution to our understanding of political theology and how it relates to the healing aspects of the gospel as well. He asserts that the test of our faithfulness is whether we live by the understanding of our faith when such commitment is costly as well as when it is advantageous.[6] Christ cannot be invoked in defense of the existing order and conveniently be considered irrelevant when that order comes under attack. Shinn cautions that church leaders will not successfully influence their constituencies to make institutional changes without addressing the consciousness that clings to outdated and even vicious institutions.[7]

He asks us to unite awareness of transcendence with awareness of incarnation. By bringing these two dimensions of our faith together, we are led to a dedication to political and social justice. Christian faith and social action are wed. We do not have the opportunity to isolate faith from politics. Christians cannot minister to men's souls as though prophecy had never called men to justice and as though Christ had never been flesh. The total meaning of faith is not exhausted in political action, as though God does not heal through his grace our troubled and mortal humanity.

Shinn sums up the case thus:

Political theology must not reduce the Christian faith to politics alone. . . . But Christian faith, in testifying that it is more than political, may not become less than political. This faith declares a good news of justice, forgiveness, liberation, and reconciliation.[8]

The Bureau of the Census reported that blacks remained far behind whites in most socioeconomic categories over a five-year period ending in 1972. In fact, there were indications that the gap was widening in some areas. In median income, the gap between black and white families of four widened due to the low income of black women, and the number of poor black families headed by females continued to climb. The unemployment ratio between the races is also rising. All these facts indicate the historical and social disparity of the races. For example, one fourth of all black families received some form of public assistance in 1971 compared to 5 percent of white families. Further, in 1971 white infant mortality was half that of blacks, even though there was a sizable decrease of this in both races.

Compare this with reports by Ben J. Watenberg and Richard M. Scamon, in April of 1973, that the majority of blacks are moving into the middle class. Although there have been some social and economic gains in recent years, most blacks have not shared in such gains.[9]

A Harvard economist, Richard B. Freeman, made an analysis of Census Bureau and Bureau of Labor Statistics reports. He noted a convergence of black and white incomes and concluded that the figures indicated "a virtual collapse in traditional discriminatory patterns in the labor market." [10]

For such a view, Freeman drew mainly upon those who have made it. He ignored the disparity between the median income of whites ($11,549) and the median income of blacks ($6,864). Some 500,000 blacks and other minorities moved into poverty in the same year (1972). It is shocking that so many other blacks moved into poverty while white Americans were moving the other way.

America is creating or perpetuating through its social and economic policy two groups among blacks: the almost equal and the abandoned. While seizing upon the good news about race relations, we are ignoring the hard realities in our ghettos. The Nixon administration, from Daniel Moynihan's "benign neglect" to Howard Phillips' dismantling of the Office of Economic Opportunity, has launched a frontal attack against social welfare programs affecting the lives of the black, the poor, and the aging. Today, as Freeman observes, one third of all blacks remain in poverty and 40 percent of all black children are poor.[11] This situation suggests

a lifetime of deep trouble for this country; the great bulk of these children will never make it to the college educated labor market class and indeed, many of them will not even make it into the labor market at all. They will remain poor, hopeless, and angry, immune to any permanent benefits which changes in the operation or structure of the labor market or strong upward thrusts in . . . the economy may bestow.[12]

In the summer of 1973, Herbert Hill, NAACP national labor director, reported that unemployment rates among young blacks had reached disaster levels. He predicted that unless the trend changes, virtually an entire generation of ghetto youth will never enter the labor force. His projections showed youth unemployment approaching 50 percent. This situation was seen by Hill as the worst since the great depression. Unemployment is indeed an explosive factor, causing urban unrest and having dangerous implications for inner city and suburb alike. The overall picture is one of racial discrimination against black workers, ranging from total exclusion in some trades to mere tokenism in others. Hill rightly observes that "neglect has now become criminal complicity." [13]

It is time for social scientists to begin to interpret figures in personal terms. Sometimes figures lie. This is especially true when the black condition in this society is lumped into the average account with all Americans. A very high percentage of blacks remain at the very bottom of this society. We are still the doormats, the "hewers of wood and drawers of water." We are like the Israelites under cruel taskmasters while in Egyptian bondage under a "law and order" Pharaoh whose heart was hardened against the oppressed. The exodus is one powerful symbol of liberation for such a time as this.

This is a very unfortunate period. There are those who assemble selected information about the status of black people and attempt to tell us how well off we are, when we know it "ain't so." When I observe people directly, rather than figures, I know that blacks in this society are hurting. When I observe black laborers at the District Line in the nation's capital seeking a day's work at a time, I know we are hurting as a people. These are husbands and fathers who get up early in the morning, who, with lunch bag in hand, go and wait in order to bargain with a white "boss" for a day's work. Only those who are willing to work hard and for little money are hired by these white exploiters. These black laborers are churchmen, community leaders, and good family men where they live. Many of the black men end up as dope addicts, drunks, and prisoners when they can't take it anymore. Skid Row, Talley's Corner, or the city jail is often their only haven. Anyone sensitive to the human condition would not rely on charts, graphs, and statistics as important as these are. Anyone with just plain common sense and a heart of compassion can see that the mass of black folk are still victims of gross injustices and inequities in this society. This is a case where the sins of omission of the fathers have overtaken many white churchgoers. It is the business of black theology to make these very churchgoers ill at ease in their racist Zion. God rejects their "appointed feasts," for their hands are "full of blood." They must first go and straighten out the broken relationship with blacks before forgiveness is available to them.

In the black-white encounter since 1954, both "conscienceless power" and "powerless conscience" have been manifest as reality and not merely as myth. The civil rights movement on the legal front was supported by a nonviolent approach directed at the white conscience. The statement of 1966 by what is now the National Committee of Black Churchmen (NCBC) referred to the period of Martin Luther King's leadership as summed up in the words "powerless conscience." Let me hasten to say that my own attitude toward Dr. King's mission is affirmative and yet not uncritical. Looking at the impact of Dr. King's unusual leadership in retrospect, and assessing the negative reaction and the indifference of white leadership to his appeal to conscience, I believe the churchmen were close to the mark. Dr. King spoke of the concept of natural law as operative in the universe and in the moral affairs of men. He believed in the redemptive power of unmerited suffering. He sounded the "trumpet of conscience" because he assumed that there is something in all men that is responsive to an appeal for love and justice. He was not sufficiently sensitive to what racism has done over a long period in corroding the conscience of white Americans. Thus, the condition which alone makes nonviolence a means to better racial understanding (a highly sensitive and morally perceptive conscience) was not evident in white America. In fact, his "I Have a Dream" speech (a political, social, ethical, and literary masterpiece) fell, as it were, on deaf ears. It was wasted on a multitude who "seeing see not"; who hear and yet do not hear.

At first many black lawyers deeply committed to the civil rights movement considered Dr. King a nuisance. He invested so much in the theological concept of eternal law and in the moral concept of natural law that they saw him as a stumbling block to positive law. Many of these lawyers, steeped in the case-precedent procedure in legal enactment, abhorred the idea that law might have theological, ethical, and philosophical foundations. Law was simply what the courts decided. When Dr. King spoke of just and unjust laws and asserted that an unjust and inhuman law is immoral and should not be obeyed even if the cost of disobedience is imprisonment or death, these lawyers became disenchanted with his ministry.

It was not long, however, before these black lawyers observed legal decisions that opposed any sense of justice or humanity. Some young Turks on the civil rights task force of the Justice Department were asked to go easy on cases they were reasonably certain they could have won. Often they were told that because of the political situation in a particular state or the power of a committee chairman in Washington, it would not be expedient to take a case to court. The black lawyers soon got the impression, and rightly so, that top officials in the national administration were playing with the freedom of blacks. Lawyers with the rights of black people at heart began to lose faith in their own craft. It was then that many began to see the importance of Dr. King's ministry and the witness of the black church in the interest of human rights, of which civil rights are a part. They perceived that Dr. King's Southern Christian Leadership Conference (SCLC) was a moral support for legal breakthroughs in the civil rights field. They began to realize how much ground-swell support the black church has among the black masses. Black lawyers started going to church and began initiating their legal actions from the pews with the full backing of preachers and congregations.

The litigation against racism became bogged down in endless court battles, legal loopholes, and all types of legal dodges. And, unfortunately, the movement led by Dr. King had not given proper theological and ethical attention to power. Dr. King did not denounce power. He considered power as being morally neutral, as did his Boston professors, but he did not give it adequate attention. He put all his confidence in *satyagraha,* "truth force," a type of moral power; but he equated it with *agape,* love, rather than with "the pushing and shoving of justice." He trusted the conscience of the white man, believing that the white conscience would be responsive to his nonviolent militant movement. Against this background the conclusion of the National Committee of Black Churchmen was correct. Dr. King did in fact sponsor a type of "powerless conscience" approach toward the alleviation of racism. What he did not fully assess was "the conscienceless power" of white

America. Because he longed for peace, he did get involved in the movement that opposed American involvement in Vietnam. Perhaps this represents his dawning awareness that America has a deep-seated insensitivity to suffering and oppression as far as people of color in the world are concerned. If he had noted the involvements of the CIA and American-based multinational corporations as well as our support of colonial and exploitative regimes in the Third World, including Latin America, he might have seen how bad the picture really is. Dr. King's observations on Vietnam did not sufficiently inform his program of combatting racism. They did not bring him to the use of power to counteract power. He relied on arousing guilt in the white conscience.

With a moral earnestness admired by all, Dr. King maintained the position that "love is the more excellent way." His was the only ethical way. He opposed black power as racism in reverse and invested all in the Poor People's Campaign. His participation in this ultimate push to vindicate pragmatically his faith in the redeeming power of undeserved suffering love was aborted by his assassination. Rather than a vindication of what Dr. King gave his life for, the effort became a disaster.

Ralph David Abernathy was an unfortunate successor to such an unusual man as Martin Luther King, Jr. Abernathy's only qualification appeared to be that he had been by Dr. King's side from the beginning. Other talented leaders in the SCLC were ignored as the mantle fell upon this ordinary man. It is sobering to note that both Andrew Young and Jesse Jackson were in the movement. Resurrection City was a tragic failure. The cold, damp weather in Washington turned the camp into a pigsty. This follows in a moral sense also. Some leaders enjoyed the luxury of plush hotels and moved in high social circles while abandoning the black and poor in what was erroneously called Resurrection City. The camp became virus- and vice-infested. The crowd was finally cleaned out by the police. The incumbent administration in Washington did not lend the oppressed an ear. Instead of a moral, or any other kind of victory, "resurrection," a symbol of victory, here wallowed in defeat. This grand effort, which might have justified Dr. King's trust in nonviolent means to racial justice and equality, did not come off. The blow sustained as a result of the Poor People's Campaign has not been overcome in SCLC, which has sustained various splits that led to the birth of other movements. People United to Save Humanity (PUSH), under Jesse Jackson, is one of the most outstanding results of these splits. All in all, Resurrection City demonstrated to many the fact that "powerless conscience" cannot successfully overcome a "conscienceless power" in this nation.

"Black Power" summed up a new consciousness, a felt need for an alternative to "nonviolence," not merely as a method but as a new way of seeing and acting to which blacks should turn for their liberation from racist oppression. We are a pragmatic people as our African forefathers were. We needed our self-respect and we needed greater results in terms of the delivery of goods and services to the masses of black Americans and not just to a few token blacks. There is a desire for personal identity, a sense of togetherness as a people, and sufficient power to bargain for our rights, not out of weakness, but out of strength.

What has been outlined is the affirmative side of black power. What erupted at first was violence in the streets.

The hot rhetoric of the late 1960's did more to create the white backlash than it did to deliver blacks from white oppression. It provided a basis for the righteous indignation of middle-class Americans to be aroused in support of sadistic cops and racist politicians. "Law and order" became a passport of high political office, including the presidency. But it was to be law and order without justice. It reminds one of what one finds in some undeveloped countries. In the government's zeal to stamp out corruption, crimes that are petty in consequences are punished by shooting or hanging the criminal; at the same time, top officials in government who steal large sums of money are punished slightly or merely asked to resign. Similarly, we are harsh with those who commit crimes among the oppressed in this society, while we wink at white-collar crime. Property is considered more valuable than persons. The poor and the blacks of this society are herded off to prisons for long periods of time without adequate attention being given to their civil rights or rehabilitation. Watergate, however, has jolted many good, decent, Christian white citizens. We are realizing that the law and order men were sending up a smoke screen to cover up their own crimes, which occurred not in the streets but in the suites of the rich and the powerful. Watergate symbolizes here at home what Vietnam illustrated abroad. The political leadership of this nation is insensitive to the masses of oppressed people at home and abroad.

The amoral or immoral stance of the national administration regarding war in Indochina and unjust treatment of minorities at home silenced a generation of morally sensitive whites. Militant peaceniks became Eastern mystics or "Jesus people." Even Jewish youth began to speak in tongues and exalt the name of Jesus. But in spite of gospel singing, blacks are still anchored in reality. We have always been able to shout in church and yet insist on earthly freedom. We refuse to flee to the wilderness or to any other nether world of the spirit. We are still in the cities and there we are involved in social and political programs for black liberation. Blacks are now aware that love and justice cannot be had without power.

A black political theology provides a theological foundation for an action-oriented people who are determined to be "black and free." This theology emerges out of the crucible of black suffering and out of the dark night of the black soul's distress. We seek the deliverance of a people as well as personal liberation. We will have the dignity of sons of God here and now. Therefore, black political theology has more to say about the salvation of blacks-in-community in this life.

IO

Liberation and
Reconciliation Revisited

Liberation theology is associated with the vigorous manner of interpreting the message and mission of Christian churches in Latin America. It resembles the theology of hope of Jürgen Moltmann. It is similar to the liberation theology of Frederick Herzog. Herzog and Rosemary Ruether are examples of white theologians who have the ability to apply the concept of liberation to a number of "causes." This is valuable if it does not move too far from the empirical realities of the oppressed. Liberation theology in Latin America and black theology in the United States are focused on real life situations as experienced by the theologians and those for whom they interpret the faith.

Liberation theology resembles the emphasis of Moltmann and Pannenberg as they attempt to reformulate the eschatological dimensions of the Biblical message and to find in the promise of the Parousia of the risen, glorified Christ and the final consummation of God's Kingdom the basis of hope. Herzog's summons to church folk to identify with the agony of "the wretched of the earth" and to "become black" is very helpful.

But there are fundamental differences between the theologians of hope and the Latin-American liberation theologians. Moltmann and Pannenberg are working within the context of Western European influences. Rubem Alves and Gustavo Gutiérrez are speaking from Brazilian and Peruvian perspectives. Moltmann and Pannenberg speak out of the secure university settings of affluent countries. Gutiérrez and Helder Camara are formulating their liberation theologies from firsthand experience through identification with the suffering masses in their countries. They speak authentically and concretely about the gospel addressing itself to dehumanizing conditions. The liberating words and actions of these theologians have the ring of truth and the weight of authority.

There is a close affinity between the mood of black theologians and the liberation theologians of Latin America because conditions giving rise to the two movements are similar. It is rather easy for black theologians to enter into dialogue with Latin-American liberation theologians because both are tuned in on an oppressed human situation. It is my view that the experience of oppression of blacks over such a long period of time has seared the conscience of most white churchgoers. Theological scholasticism, pietism, moralism, and evangelicalism obtain, but there is little attention given to justice, love, and mercy in the social field. There is less concern for making life more human for those outside one's racial or ethnic group. It is conveniently asserted that politics and religion do not mix. This makes it possible for preachers to preach and for churchgoers to worship in peace, while businessmen exploit and politicians do as they please. It is no great surprise to find white Americans involved in Watergate, in

Vietnam, or in international exploitation of the poor in the Third World. The same racist inhumanity that has characterized the treatment of blacks at home has now been transported abroad.

We must not ignore the differences in the contexts of liberation theology and black theology. The liberation theologians are in Latin America, where Roman Catholicism is predominant. They are in "developing countries," the governments are often totalitarian, and the masses are often influenced by some aspect of Marxism. Church and state are often united in a bond with foreign governments and multinational corporations to exploit the masses. Liberation movements are often violent, and the task is to overthrow the existing social order to make way for a more humane order. Looking now at black theology, we note that it is mainly Protestant. The Roman Catholic Church in the United States has not groomed any major black theologians. The majority of blacks are not Roman Catholic anyway. Black theologians live in a developed and pluralistic society. In some ways this makes the awareness of oppression more intense. Ours is more of a race problem than a class problem. The suffering of the black poor is very widespread and intense, however. Between black Americans and the masses of people in Latin America is a fellowship of those who bear the mark of pain. Black theologians are not bound by church dogmas; neither do they seek church approval for their reflections. They are not spokesmen for any denomination. Latin-American theologies are more dependent upon theologies of hope that are being developed in Europe and among white American theologians and that stem directly from a Christian-Marxist dialogue.

Black theology is ecumenical. It is seeking to be indigenous by rooting itself in the African/Afro-American religious heritage. We also lift up meaning and protest as twin foci in our religious heritage. Ours has been an experience of suffering without bitterness. But out of this crucible has emerged a robust faith that now deserves theological interpretation. We have discovered deep in our African roots the basis for sharing and caring in the notion of "familyhood" in African society. We note a sense of servanthood, togetherness, and stewardship in primitive Christianity and our religious heritage. In sum, liberation theologies and black theology are expressions of theological ethics. Both are political theologies in that they reject the privatization of the gospel and insist that the focus of theology move from personal anxieties to social, economic, and political responsibility. With the exception of James Cone's, existent programs in black theology belong to "soft theologies of revolution." They do not advocate violence as either pragmatic or ethical. On the other hand, liberation programs in Latin America for the most part take violence for granted as the only pragmatic or ethical ground for hope.[1]

White racism has been aptly described by Buell H. Gallagher as follows:

> The attitudes of whites, ranging from friendly paternalism to hatred and hostility, tend to recognize a caste status in which all whites are in one way or another superior to all Negroes, who in turn must in no respect be superior to any whites.[2]

The conclusion he reaches is sound:

> The caste system is an established part of American culture, with clear legal and social definitions . . . with general characteristics of similarity in all parts of the nation. This is the caste system that confronts and confuses the Christian conscience.[3]

Robert W. Terry addresses himself to what he calls "a new white consciousness"—an awareness of whiteness and its role in race relations. American culture is color-conscious. To dissociate oneself from whiteness ignores what whiteness has done for those who are white and against those who are not. Racism is not just the consciousness of color, but what is done with that consciousness. The American experience has not been identical for blacks and whites. Whites have been the perpetrators and beneficiaries of white racism; blacks have been the victims. Whites are often unaware that whiteness is a problem. On the other hand, blacks discover early in life that whiteness is a problem with which they must deal.

Whiteness cannot be denied by efforts to be black. There is no neutral ground, for whites participate in racist institutions which dehumanize black life. The new white consciousness reminds whites of what is needed to reconstruct a different understanding of the meaning of whiteness as well as what needs to be done to make the lot of nonwhite persons better. Only as whites see themselves as the real problem will they begin to work at causes instead of symptoms.[4]

According to Terry, racism is individual, institutional, and cultural. The cultural expression of racism is the most difficult to conquer. As long as cultural racism exists, there will be individual and institutional expression of racism.

Whites assume a color-plus understanding of racism. A black is black plus lazy, plus immoral, plus militant. The color-plus response makes it difficult for many whites to recognize and admit that they are racist.[5]

Racism is any activity by individuals, groups, institutions, or cultures that treats human beings unjustly because of color and rationalizes that treatment by attributing to them undesirable biological, psychological, social, or cultural characteristics.[6]

The task for those with the new white consciousness carries with it a different life-style. The following program is proposed: Whites should (1) become conscious agents of change; (2) seek ethical clarity; (3) identify the many forms and expressions of white racism; (4) develop social strategies for change to eliminate and move beyond racism; (5) discern the appropriate tactics—assess their power to change; and (6) experiment, test, and refine personal life-styles consistent with these newly affirmed values.[7]

Those who are informed by the "new white consciousness" are to become "intentionally political." They are to use power creatively and justly and engage in "intelligent reflection." They are to "develop credentials" by attacking racism in white-dominated structures. Credentials come from involvement in fighting racism. All along the way there must be "progressive listening." This leads to "shared meaning" with blacks. Thus the foundation for growth and change is laid. From Terry's personal conviction based on his personal experiences in Detroit, he believes that the white community has a desperate need and opportunity to develop a new white conscience and that there is a growing readiness for this.[8] Let us hope that his optimism is based on fact. We are agreed that the sharing and the humanizing of white power is a Christian responsibility. Terry is correct in asserting that the "new white" committed to justice and working to rid this nation of its racism can be a major force in social change for better race relations.

Sterling Tucker addressed blacks in a constructive way similar to Terry's address to whites. As a "moderate militant," Tucker seeks to work within the system to humanize it. Separatism, like integration with its tokenism, legal dodges, and moral paralysis, is a one-way street. As a means to achieve a specific task, separatism may be useful, but as a goal it leads to disaster. The psychological benefits of black nationalism have been like tonic to our soul. We have received strength, dignity, self-confidence, and self-affirmation from it. Tucker indicates how separatism has unmasked the myths and illusions of token integration. But what we want and need is not blackness alone; it is the freedom of free men.

To this end we will need to enter into temporary ad hoc alliances with other interest groups—i.e., Indians or Hispanic groups. In the cooperative alliances no ideological unity would be sought. There would be cooperation on issues. It must be acknowledged that at one time a special interest group may join forces with blacks, but at another time the interest of the other group may run counter to our interest. Blacks must not allow themselves to be co-opted while recognizing that numbers count in getting things done. What Tucker is seeking is a means to move blacks from the rapping to the planning or programming stage of the liberation struggle.

The anger that resounded in the call for black power

now feeds a sense of powerlessness. The rage of the riots now is turned inward. One should note the high suicide rates among black males between twenty and thirty-five, together with the wanton killing of blacks by blacks. As whites and middle-class blacks vacate the inner city, a stark helplessness is settling in on the black poor. There is, however, a great power potential among the black poor because of their number. Effective community organization under a new type of leadership is their only hope.

The grass-roots leadership supported by a genuine fellowship can move City Hall. A greater responsiveness to the needs of the black poor is being forced upon black leadership. Black leaders can no longer be a palliative. They must now become advocates. The hand-picked black leaders who served as symbolic figures or ceremonial leaders are no longer welcomed by blacks who have said good-by to Uncle Tom. Blacks are rightly seeking leadership "of the people." We now need a leadership that is more than puppets or creations of the white establishment and media. We need a new leadership with a new authority and freedom promoted *by* and *for* the liberation of black people.

The black middle class has a new responsibility that is much broader. We must have in view the liberation not merely of ourselves but of all our brothers and sisters. We must inspire faith in the future and prepare all our people for movement into it. We must discover our strengths and make maximum use of the resources we have. Anger must be used constructively. We must get ourselves together and do with and for ourselves what only we can do. Tucker has a tendency to write off the church because he sees the black community as issue-oriented. To me, as a church-

man and theologian, there is convincing evidence apparent
to indicate that the black church remains the strongest
tower of strength available for black liberation. What the
black church needs is leadership, a political theology and
a plan of action.

Harvey Cox makes a very important suggestion when
he asserts that in Jesus of Nazareth we encounter a God
who discloses himself through activities that threatens the
status quo, through something like revolution. God's word
for the world is a lived word, Jesus of Nazareth. God
touches and renews the world through the Incarnate Life.
Jesus is the real sacrament and our participation in the
sacrificial action of God in Christ is true discipleship. This
is to share in God's suffering in the world today. The ministry of the church is participation in this mission of God.
It is the task of the church to find out where God is on the
move in the world today and hasten to join him. Through
the life of Jesus we are aware that God and world belong
together.[9] Cox agrees with Bonhoeffer's assertion: "It is
only in the midst of the world that Christ is Christ." [10]

Thus far Cox moves in the direction in which the present writer sees black theology moving. But then he goes
secular and juxtaposes secularism and religiousness.[11]
He views even the servanthood of Jesus in secular terms.
He calls for a nonreligious ministry. In his earlier works
Cox attempted to downgrade the significance of cultic
worship, otherworldliness, and the like to make room for
his secularization pitch. He was even willing to reverse the
relation between secular and sacred to establish a priority
for the secular. He wanted to make the point that God's
word to us is a living deed, a life lived, hands working and
feet walking among us. From the perspective of black the-

ology, the price he pays for his religionless, secularized gospel is unnecessary and too high. In our purview we can have an understanding of the gospel which offers personal and social salvation without secularizing the sacred or sacralizing the secular. The gospel is for the whole man and for all of life.

Cox is helpful, however, at other points. He describes sloth, *acedia,* as a cardinal moral evil. It is said to be a cardinal sin or a source sin leading to a structural derangement that breeds other sins. Through *acedia,* a man renounces the claim to his human dignity—he does not will his own being. Since sloth is such a fertile sin, it tempts man to other expressions of inhumanity against God's purpose for human life. Man is to affirm and celebrate life. He is to accept and decide who he will be. A man is not to accept stereotypes assigned to him. He is required to open his eyes to observe how power is distributed and exercised in society. He is to assume a full measure of the pain and responsibility that goes with the uses of power. To shirk these privileges and responsibilities is to commit the sin of *acedia,* to lapse into sloth. We cannot hold on to our humanity if we allow others to dictate the identities with which we live out our lives. Sloth has political dimensions also, for man's existence is by its very nature life with and for the fellowman. Thus, the apathetic avoidance of politics is one way to club the weak and powerless brother to death. We abdicate our assignment as stewards. The gospel calls us, according to Cox, to adult stewardship, originality, inventiveness, and the governance of the world.

Cox has challenged the black man to affirm his authentic existence by getting rid of any false self-image imposed upon him by his oppressor. He is to lay claim to his authentic selfhood bestowed upon him by the Creator, Redeemer, and Sanctifier of human life. He has challenged the white Christian to humanize "white power" by assuming the stewardship of his new humanity in Christ. Both have a responsibility to be about God's liberating work in the world.

While not identifying with the seventeenth-century Puritans or with the Society of Friends, black theologians may profit from a critical look at the way these Christian groups have seen God at work in the world. Their insight and example may indicate to some extent how a political theology has supported radical social transformation.

The Puritans were the Bolsheviks of their time. They fought and won a long and bloody civil war and established a viable regime. They instituted a new social, political, and economic order. They even exported their revolution and subverted neighboring governments. To the Puritans, politics and religion were one.

The Puritans placed a lot of emphasis upon Christian faith in history. God loved the world and we have as our mission social salvation as well as personal salvation. Government should reflect religion and serve its purposes. Their political theology was covenant theology. God in his concern to redeem the world elected to do this by gathering a people to himself through which he would accomplish his work of salvation. The Old Testament records God's covenant with the Jews. In his covenant he promised to be their God and they agreed to be his people. This covenant was supported by the "steadfast love" of God and was to be sealed by the faithfulness of Israel. The Old Covenant with the Jews opened up the way for the New Covenant through Christ. The Puritans thought of themselves as the exclusive people of God, expressly gathered for the purpose of doing his work in history.

The Puritans discovered covenant theology by reading Scripture in the light of Calvin's *Institutes*. They felt that they were better able to understand and apply the Biblical message through this theology. For them the Bible was a blueprint for organizing church and state, and it became their manual for action here and now. While there are perils as well as promises in the Puritan position, it does have the advantage of getting Christians involved in the transformation of society. The real task is to give proper ethical direction to such an action-oriented expression of faith. Those chosen of God are to be about his liberating work in the world, but are not to proceed by enslavement or physical destruction of their former oppressors.

Another version of a theology of involvement is that which motivates the Quakers, or Society of Friends. The Friends rejected the Calvinism of the Puritans but retained their revolutionary thrust. And again they sought radical social transformation by nonviolent means. The political thrust of covenant theology is present, but the Friends sought a deeper grasp of the New Covenant in the context of Puritan covenantism. Christ had come to lead his people himself, and the New Covenant was a living, dialogic relationship. As the people of God, the Friends were gathered into communities of discipleship, or "meetings." The model for any Christian community was, as they viewed it, the original band of twelve disciples. Like that chosen few, the community of discipleship engaged itself continually in hearing and obeying its leader. Christ sat at the head of the meeting. Leadership in the New Covenant was prophetic just as it had been in the Old Covenant. Christ as head of the fellowship is prophet as well as priest.

The Friends knew that what they were doing really mattered in world history. It was their understanding that God is Lord of creation and history and that he gathered them as a people for action here and now. Their revolutionary vision was critical of the existing social order. They had in their purview a world radically different from the present order. That is to say, they were not comfortable with the *status quo*. They were "outsiders," at least in their inner life and social vision. They saw the need for communities dedicated to a revolutionary faithfulness aimed at a new humanity and a new society. This corporateness of Quakerism is especially useful for black Christians to adopt at this time, afflicted as we are by the breakdown of community.

Christ is embraced as a divine leader and he is the one who inspires them to faithfulness. Faithfulness to his Lordship is the support for their theology and ethics. Relying on him, Friends helped one another; by sharing their burdens they made them lighter. They were governed by their loyalty to Christ more than they were by deeds and rules. In this way they developed a revolutionary program for radical social change. They produced in their midst prophetic leadership, but at the same time they assumed that the community is wiser and holier than the sum of its parts. In a real sense, Quakers believe that "the Kingdom of God is within." They have lived a "realized eschatology" —living *now* as though the Kingdom were already present. The life-style of the community, the meeting, witnessed to a new social order, the New Covenant, and a new humanity.[12]

Jan M. Lochman of Czechoslovakia reminds us that

theology can easily become an ideological justification of the establishment giving support to the concern for the "law and order" of the *status quo*. He calls such theology at its best a "Sleeping Beauty" and at its worst "the opiate of the people." [13] This Constantinian type of theology cannot move engaged Christians in a revolutionary age. But there is another type of theology, a theology of the exodus and of change, which does not water down action. At its center is the event of liberation through obedience. It is concerned about light for action through a vision of faith. It desires to keep action truly human.[14]

> There is also the theology of the biblical prophets and apostles, an intellectual network of the fishermen. . . . In its *form*, it is a biblical theology, the thought of the exodus, concerned about God's commitment to man in history, trying in thought and action to interpret this commitment into the perplexities of history and society today. In its *approach*, it is a theology of dialogue—the dialectical thought of pilgrims who do not claim ready-made dogmas and blueprints but who think and live as Socratic evangelists in honest give-and-take with their fellow pilgrims. In its *social perspective*, it is a theology of the Kingdom and of its righteousness, challenging all the justice and injustice of human laws and orders and opening the possibilities for creative change.[15]

Black political theology is not cast in the mold of the Marxist-Christian dialogue, but it has something in common with Lochman. There is a conscious effort to provide a theology for liberation for individual Christians and black churches.

Black theology has a special contribution to make to the Christian understanding of reconciliation. Love in

Christian context for the black Christian is to be applied *horizontally* as well as *vertically*. In fact, it cannot be genuine Christian love if it is not *ethical* as well as *spiritual*. There can be no unilateral expression of love between man and God which does not include the brother. Furthermore, the expression of Christian love must be particular, concrete, and personal. Christian reconciliation cannot be based upon an abstract leap to a universal concept of man. The "Fatherhood of God and brotherhood of man" formula belongs to the era of integration rather than liberation. It was possible to love everybody during this period without being a good Samaritan—without personalizing one's compassion for a person in black skin. Love could be demonstrated through "handouts" without altering the relationship of whites over blacks, without sharing and humanizing power. Apart from brotherhood week and the worship that gave sanction to it, it was business as usual for good white Christians who received benefits from a society that systematically oppresses the black and the poor.

Though we may agree that those who oppress have a greater responsibility in bringing about reconciliation, it is for the oppressed to raise the issue as to the terms upon which reconciliation is possible. It is also likely that only the oppressed can appreciate fully the real meaning of reconciliation. The "more excellent way," the way of reconciling love, includes the affirmation of authentic selfhood, the self-respect that results from a new self-understanding. Being aware of the wholeness of life, of the unity of faith and ethics and of the equity built into the assurances we have through God's revelation in nature and grace, leads to a richer understanding of God's reconciling work in the world through Christ as well as the Christian's vocation of reconciliation as a co-worker with God.

Reconciliation is always to be placed in conjunction with liberation. What we seek is a liberating experience of reconciliation. The God who sets us free from the enslavement of sin is the one who promises an abundant life to the whole man. A black political theology is not based upon a sentimental love or "cheap grace." It rests upon a firm foundation of faith in a God who suffers with "these his little ones," but who has power to set his people free, even from sin and death. But the Lord of life also heals the brokenness that separates men and nations. It is an urgent responsibility thrust upon us that we seek to "heal our land" by purging it of racism. In this matter as in all others, judgment begins at the house of God.

Martin Luther King, Jr., was correct: "We can't wait!" We must actively seek our liberation. In the churches as well as in secular power structures, we face "conscienceless power," which continues to dehumanize black people. We must develop social, economic, and political resources and use these to empower our people for their own liberation. Black churches must support black banks that have a social consciousness and that seek to aid the black poor in their economic development. We must support our black political leaders on the local front as well as strengthen and support those seeking aid for us in Congress. The black church must see as its God-given mission the liberation of the oppressed. While we continue to celebrate on Sunday morning through song and sermon, we must involve ourselves en masse to set our people free, using all the resources available in our corporate life as the body of Christ. Only in this way may we minister to the whole man and only thus may we have a liberating experience of reconciliation. It may be that in this way we may be God's instrument in the world to lead the church to be the church.

The incorporation of reconciliation into a black theology needs no justification. Reconciliation is an integral part of the gospel. Reconciliation is the very essence of the good news. God in Christ is reconciling in the world and Christians are called to be agents of this reconciling gospel. The "whole" gospel includes reconciliation. The revelation of God includes what "ought to be" and what "must be" as well as what "is." Racism, by developing a cleavage between blacks and whites, renders the gospel of no effect. The gospel is only accepted fully where the "walls of partition" are broken down between man and man. There are no exceptions. Reconciliation in our social climate includes a "cross" for all Christians, black and white. The cross for whites is repentance based upon the full awareness of what "whiteness" means in a society where whites are beneficiaries and blacks are victims. To recognize that racism is personal, institutional, and social and that all whites are sponsors of the evils of racist oppression, is a real test of the seriousness with which whites must now take their faith. For blacks, racism and the separation associated with it is an involuntary burden. Being victims of the injustices and the inhumanity resulting from racism, blacks face a real challenge when asked to extend the possibility of reconciliation to the oppressor. Our cross is forgiveness. It is only by reassessing the Christian experience of forgiveness that the foolishness of the gospel begins to speak to the black Christian. All men are one in their sin, and God, out of his abundant grace, has forgiven us. This has happened not because we have deserved it, but because God loves us out of an everlasting love. But God's grace is a "costly grace." The cross is the arch-symbol of our faith. There is no forgiveness from God unless we confess our sins. God's grace is available, but it is not automatic.

For whites to expect blacks to be reconciled to them under oppressive conditions, while they themselves continue to disregard the humanity of the black man, is inhuman and unchristian. Reconciliation can only take place when blacks as well as whites are free to affirm their authentic selfhood and peoplehood. There can be no Christian reconciliation between oppressors and the oppressed. We are called to Christian maturity in the body of Christ. The new humanity in the fellowship of believers requires that all God's children be *free* and *equal*. Only in this new relationship of *equity* will whites cease to have an investment in the misery of the black poor and only then will the black poor be liberated to be true sons of God. Only in a relationship of equity are blacks able to rise to their authentic selfhood and experience the liberty of a saving relationship with God in Christ. There can be no liberation without reconciliation and no reconciliation without liberation. The only Christian way in race relations is a liberating experience of reconciliation for the white oppressor as well as for the black oppressed. This is what a black political theology is all about, and its message is to the whole church of Christ.

Notes

INTRODUCTION

1. I have written a critical review of Herzog's *Liberation Theology* (The Seabury Press, 1972) in *Religious Education,* Vol. LXVIII, No. 4 (July–Aug., 1973), pp. 518–521. Rosemary Radford Ruether, a colleague of mine, has provided a thoughtful chapter on black theology in her *Liberation Theology: Human Hope Confronts Christian History and American Power* (Paulist/Newman Press, 1972), pp. 127–144. G. Clarke Chapman, Jr., has done a very helpful critique on James Cone's program in "American Theology in Black," *Cross Currents,* Vol. XXII, No. 2 (Spring, 1972), pp. 139–157. These references indicate that black theology is being taken seriously by representative white theologians and that a fruitful conversation is on the way.

Chapter 1

FOUNDATIONS

1. See James H. Cone, *A Black Theology of Liberation* (J. B. Lippincott Company, 1970), pp. 82–106.

2. From Archbishop William Temple, *Nature, Man and God*, quoted in J. Deotis Roberts, Sr., *From Puritanism to Platonism in Seventeenth Century England* (The Hague: Martinus Nijhoff, 1969), p. 253.

3. See Charles H. Long, "Perspectives for a Study of Afro-American Religion in the United States," *History of Religion*, Vol. II, No. 1 (Aug., 1971), pp. 54–66. See the introduction to Long's *Alpha: The Myths of Creation* (Collier Books, 1969), pp. 1–35.

4. Paulo Freire, *Pedagogy of the Oppressed*, tr. by Myra B. Ramos (Herder & Herder, Inc., 1970).

5. Gustavo Gutiérrez, *A Theology of Liberation*, tr. and ed. by Sr. Caridad Inda and John Eagleson (Orbis Books, 1972).

6. Richard R. Niebuhr, *Experiential Religion* (Harper & Row, Publishers, Inc., 1972).

7. E. Bolaji Idowu, *Towards an Indigenous Church* (Ibadan: Oxford University Press, 1965), p. 2.

8. *Ibid.*, pp. 11–15.

9. Raymond Panikkar, *The Unknown Christ of Hinduism* (London: Darton, Longman & Todd, Ltd., 1964), p .11.

10. For a fuller discussion, see *Northeast Asia Journal of Theology*, March, 1973, pp. 56–59. Also read James M. Phillips' helpful paragraph in the same journal (pp. 62–63). Prof. Phillips, an American whom I met in 1964 in Tokyo, is one who has a deep understanding of the thought and faith of Christians in the Far East.

11. See William Jones, "Theodicy: The Controlling Category for Black Theology," *Journal of Religious Thought*, Vol. XXX, No. 1 (Spring–Summer, 1973), pp. 28–38. Actually, Jones is developing a program with a balance between method and content. He is forging a very important position in black theology. His position is what he calls a "humanotheism," which addresses many black intellectuals more forcefully than any existing program in black theology.

12. I am able to report this with a degree of authority as chairman of the theologians section of the 1973 workshop sponsored by the Society for the Study of Black Religion.

13. Walter H. Capps, *Time Invades the Cathedral: Tensions in the School of Hope* (Fortress Press, 1972).

14. Johannes Pedersen, *Israel: Its Life and Culture*, 2 vols. (Oxford University Press, 1926, 1940).

15. For a profound definition and description of "symbol" as Tillich uses the word in his theology, see Paul Tillich, *Dynamics of Faith* (Harper & Brothers, 1957), pp. 41–43.

16. Everett M. Stowe, *Communicating Reality Through Symbols* (The Westminster Press, 1966), pp. 15–16.

17. Ladislas Segy, *African Sculpture*, as cited by Stowe, *op. cit.*, pp. 83–84.

18. I have been greatly helped in arriving at this position on "image-thinking" by a series of lectures delivered by my former professor, Dr. John McIntyre. The lectures were entitled "Theology and the Imagination" and were delivered by him at Union Theological Seminary in Virginia during July, 1973.

Chapter 2

ETHNICITY AND THEOLOGY

1. Martin E. Marty, "Ethnicity: The Skeleton of Religion in America," *Church History,* Vol. XLI, No. 1 (March, 1972), pp. 5–21. Cf. the use of "peoplehood" in Milton M. Gordon, *Assimilation in American Life* (Oxford University Press, 1964).

2. Cf. my "The Black Caucus and the Failure of Christian Theology," *Journal of Religious Thought,* Vol. XXVI, No. 2 (Summer, 1969), pp. 15–25.

3. Gordon, *op. cit.,* pp. 24–25. Cf. E. K. Francis, "The Nature of the Ethnic Group," *American Journal of Sociology,*

Vol. LII, No. 5 (March, 1947), pp. 393–400, and Robert Redfield, "The Folk Society," *American Journal of Sociology*, Vol. LII, No. 4 (Jan., 1947), 293–308.

4. Gordon, *op. cit.*, p. 23.

5. *Nexus*, Vol. XVI, No. 1 (Winter, 1972–73), pp. 8–19.

6. *Ibid.*, p. 11. Marty observes that "the black revolution triggered or was concurrent with other expressions of peoplehood" (Marty, *loc. cit.*, p. 5).

7. See Melville J. Herskovits, *The New World Negro*, ed. by Frances S. Herskovits (Minerva Press, 1969), pp. 114–122.

8. I have given considerable attention to this matter pro and con elsewhere. See my "African Religion and Social Consciousness," *Journal of Religious Thought*, Vol. XXIX, No. 1 (1972), pp. 43–56, and "Africanisms and Spiritual Strivings," *ibid.*, Vol. XXX, No. 1 (1973), pp. 16–27.

9. From an unpublished paper by George B. Thomas, entitled "Black Theology and Black Religion," delivered Nov. 14, 1970, in Atlanta.

10. W. H. Grier and P. M. Cobbs, *The Jesus Bag* (McGraw-Hill Book Co., Inc., 1971). They see religion as an enslaving force. They equate religion with bigotry. They embrace what they call *black morality* or the capacity for greatness. Blacks, according to these writers, "have taken a Jesus Bag shaped like a noose and refashioned it into a black cornucopia of spiritual riches" (p. 180).

11. James H. Cone, *The Spirituals and the Blues* (The Seabury Press, 1972), p. 31.

12. John Lovell, Jr., "The Social Implications of the Spirituals," *Journal of Negro Education*, Vol. VIII, No. 4 (Oct., 1939), pp. 640–641.

13. William C. Stuttles, Jr., "African Religious Survivals as Factors in American Slave Revolts," *Journal of Negro History*, Vol. LVI, No. 2 (April, 1971), p. 99.

14. Vincent Harding, "Religion and Resistance Among An-

tebellum Negroes," in August Meier and Elliott Rudwick (eds.), *The Making of Black America* (Atheneum Publishers, 1969), pp. 179–197.

15. I have written concerning this in "Folklore and Religion: The Black Experience," *Journal of Religious Thought,* Vol. XXVII, No. 2 (1970), pp. 5–15.

16. Charles L. Helton, "The Tragic in Black Historical Experience," *The Duke Divinity School Review,* Vol. XXXVIII, No. 2 (Spring, 1973), pp. 79–80.

17. James H. Cone, "Black Power, Black Theology, and the Study of Theology and Ethics," *Theological Education,* Vol. VI, No. 3 (1970), p. 209.

Chapter 3

THE WHOLENESS OF MAN

1. Genesis 2:7, KJV. Cf. the account of the creation of man in an African society, "An African Story of the Creation of Man, from the Shilluk, a Nilotic People," in Mircea Eliade (ed.), *From Primitives to Zen: A Thematic Sourcebook of the History of Religions* (Harper & Row, Publishers, Inc., 1967), pp. 137–138.

2. I have treated the "dignity" of man in my *Liberation and Reconciliation: A Black Theology* (The Westminster Press, 1971), pp. 100–108. In *From Puritanism to Platonism,* pp. 83–84, I have discussed the "image" of God in man.

3. H. Shelton Smith, *In His Image, But . . . Racism in Southern Religion, 1780–1910* (Duke University Press, 1972). Smith documents profusely the many ways in which major white Christian bodies betrayed the black man.

4. Swailem Sidhom, "The Theological Estimate of Man," in Kwesi Dickson & Paul Ellingworth (eds.), *Biblical Revelation and African Beliefs* (Orbis Books, 1969), pp. 99–104.

5. John S. Mbiti, *African Religions and Philosophy* (Frederick A. Praeger, Inc., Publishers, 1969), p. 92.

6. See C. L. Shanks, "The Biblical Anti-Slavery Argument of the Decade 1830–1840," *Journal of Negro History*, Vol. XVI (1931), pp. 132–157. This fine essay presents the proslavery theological arguments as well as those which are antislavery.

7. June Adamson, "Mary," *Christian Century*, Feb. 11, 1970, pp. 175–176. O. Kendall White, Jr.'s essay "Mormon Neo-Orthodox Theology," *Journal of Religious Thought*, Vol. XXVIII/2 (1971), pp. 119–131, is disappointing. The essay resulted from a paper given at Howard University's School of Religion in the 1971 Institute of Religion and was published in the journal of the same school. Racism is so entangled with Mormon theology, with special reference to the doctrine of man, that it was the responsibility of White in this select company to cast light upon this matter. A pure theological discussion of the difference between traditional and neo-orthodox Mormon theology before blacks at this time of black consciousness is not merely an improper scholarly omission; it is really an insult.

8. The quotation is from Stanley M. Elkins, *Slavery: A Problem in American Institutional and Intellectual Life* (University of Chicago Press, 1959). Quoted by Robert T. Handy, "Negro Christianity and American Church Historiography," in Jerald C. Brauer (ed.), *Reinterpretation in American Church History*, Essays in Divinity, Vol. V (University of Chicago Press, 1968), p. 93. Handy indicates a remarkable sensitivity as he outlines the way in which omission of the religion of blacks can be made in church history studies.

9. Gabriel Setiloane, "About Black Theology," *A New Look at Christianity in Africa, WSCF Book II/2* (Geneva, 1972), p. 69.

10. Quoted by Handy, *loc. cit.*, p. 104.

11. From the prologue of Ralph Ellison, *Invisible Man*

(New American Library of World Literature, Inc., 1952).

12. James Baldwin, "Fifth Avenue, Uptown," in Eric and Mary Josephson (eds.), *Man Alone: Alienation in Modern Society* (Dell Publishing Co., Inc., 1963), p. 355.

13. Quoted by Timothy L. Smith in "Slavery and Theology," *Church History,* Vol. XXXI, No. 4 (Dec., 1972), p. 510.

14. Joel Kovel, *White Racism: A Psychohistory* (Vintage Books, Random House, Inc., 1971), pp. 54–55.

15. *Ibid.,* pp. 65–66.

16. *Ibid.,* p. 3.

17. *Ibid.,* p. 5.

18. William H. Grier and Price M. Cobbs, *Black Rage* (Basic Books, Inc., Publishers, 1968), pp. 49–50.

19. *Ibid.,* p. 50.

20. *Ibid.,* p. 52.

21. *Ibid.,* p. 53.

22. *Ibid.,* p. 54.

23. *Ibid.,* pp. 54–55.

24. Timothy L. Smith, *loc. cit.,* p. 512.

25. See Ernst Bloch, *Man on His Own: Essays in the Philosophy of Religion,* tr. by E. B. Ashton (Herder and Herder, 1971). I have much appreciation for this work and what it contributes to our understanding of human group life. His observations on Christianity are very constructive and serve as a corrective to much personal religion that does not attack social evils.

26. Cone, *A Black Theology of Liberation,* p. 170.

27. Ken Richardson and David Spears (eds.), *Race and Intelligence* (Penguin Books, Inc., 1972), pp. 68 ff.

28. J. Garfield Owens, *All God's Chillun: Meditations on Negro Spirituals* (Abingdon Press, 1971), p. 15.

29. Timothy Smith, *loc. cit.,* pp. 502–503.

30. Robert Moats Miller, "The Protestant Churches and Lynching, 1919–1939," *Journal of Negro History* (1928), p. 118.

31. Quoted in *ibid.*

32. "A Litany at Atlanta," in Abraham Chapman (ed.), *Black Voices: An Anthology of Afro-American Literature* (New American Library of World Literature, Inc., 1968), p. 361.

33. *Ibid.*, p. 360.

34. *Ibid.*, pp. 360–361.

35. Howard Thurman, *The Search for Common Ground* (Harper & Row, Publishers, Inc., 1971), p. 24.

36. Julius K. Nyerere, *Ujamaa—Essays on Socialism* (Dar es Salaam: Oxford University Press, 1970), p. 12.

37. Margret Shannon, "Here Comes Billy Graham," *Atlanta Constitution Magazine*, June 17, 1973.

38. *Atlanta Constitution,* June 18, 1973.

Chapter 4

THE PAIN AND POWER OF GOD

1. Rubem A. Alves, *A Theology of Human Hope* (Corpus Books, 1969), p. 116.

2. William Jones, "Theodicy: The Controlling Category for Black Theology," *Journal of Religious Thought,* Vol. XXXII (1973), p. 28. Jones quotes Moltmann with approval, *ibid.*, pp. 28–29 (n. 3).

3. Jürgen Moltmann, *Religion, Revolution and the Future,* tr. by M. Douglas Meeks (Charles Scribner's Sons, 1969), p. 205.

4. Thomas W. Ogletree, "The Gospel as Power: Explorations in a Theology of Social Change," in Martin E. Marty and Dean G. Peerman (eds.), *New Theology No. 8* (The Macmillan Company, 1971), p. 175.

5. Nathan Wright, Jr., *Black Power and Urban Unrest: Creative Possibilities* (Hawthorn Books, Inc., 1968), p. 136.

6. *Ibid.*

7. John Macquarrie, "How Is Theology Possible?" in Martin E. Marty and Dean G. Peerman (eds.), *New Theology No. 1* (The Macmillan Company, 1964), pp. 21–33.

8. *Ibid.*, p. 30.

9. Kazoh Kitamori, *Theology of the Pain of God* (John Knox Press, 1958).

10. Carl Michalson, *Japanese Contributions to Christian Theology* (The Westminster Press, 1960), p. 73.

11. *Ibid.*, p. 77.

12. *Ibid.*, p. 80.

13. Meyer Fortes, "Oedipus and Job in West African Religion," in Charles M. Leslie (ed.), *Anthropology of Folk Religion* (Vantage Press, Inc., 1960), pp. 15, 49.

14. E. Bolaji Idowu, "God," in Dickson and Ellingworth (eds.), *Biblical Revelation and African Beliefs*, p. 28.

15. Countee Cullen, "Yet Do I Marvel" in Chapman, *op. cit.*, p. 383.

16. Gene Rice, "The Curse That Never Was," *Journal of Religious Thought*, Vol. XXIX, No. 1 (1972), p. 19.

17. Gustaf Wingren, *An Exodus Theology: Einar Billing and the Development of Modern Swedish Theology*, tr. by Eric Wahlstrom (Fortress Press, 1969), p. 32.

18. Albert C. Outler, *Who Trusts in God: Musings on the Meaning of Providence* (Oxford University Press, 1967), p. 95.

19. Douglas J. Hall, "Hope Against Hope," *WSCF Book 3* (Geneva, 1971), p. 31.

20. *Ibid.*, pp. 32–33.

21. From W. E. B. Du Bois, "A Litany at Atlanta," in Chapman, *op. cit.*, p. 360.

22. Charles Crowe, "Racial Violence and Social Reform— Origins of the Atlanta Riot of 1906," *Journal of Negro History*, Vol. XXXII, 1957.

23. Sidney Kaplan, "Herman Melville and the American National Sin," *Journal of Negro History*, Vol. XXXII (1957), pp. 11–37. Cf. James H. Smylie, "Uncle Tom's Cabin Re-

visited," *Interpretation,* Vol. XXVII, No. 1 (1973), pp. 67–85.

24. An excellent book on theodicy in its classical expression is John H. Hick, *Evil and the God of Love* (Harper & Row, Publishers, Inc., 1966). Cf. Francis M. Young, "Insight or Incoherence? The Greek Fathers on God and Evil," *Journal of Ecclesiastical History,* Vol. XXIV, No. 2 (April, 1973), pp. 113–126. A former student of mine, Henry T. Simmons, has begun a serious study of the theodicy issue in black religious experience. He has taken seriously the history of black religion and has given special attention to the spirituals. See "Theodicy and Hope in Black Theology," unpublished M.Div. thesis, School of Religion, Howard University, 1972.

25. Arthur Miller, *The Creation of the World and Other Business: A Play* (The Viking Press, Inc., 1973).

26. James Weldon Johnson, "Let My People Go," *God's Trombones,* p. 52.

27. William M. Philpot, *Best Black Sermons* (Judson Press, 1972), p. 6.

Chapter 5

JESUS MEANS FREEDOM

1. Joseph R. Washington, Jr., *Black Religion: The Negro and Christianity in the United States* (Beacon Press, 1964), pp. 145–148.

2. Howard Thurman, *Jesus and the Disinherited* (Abingdon-Cokesbury Press, 1949).

3. Washington, *op. cit.,* p. 216.

4. See Albert B. Cleage, Jr., *The Black Messiah* (Sheed & Ward, Inc., 1969). I made my response to this work in my *Liberation and Reconciliation.* My own interpretation of this concept also appears in Ch. VI of that volume.

5. S. G. F. Brandon, *Jesus and the Zealots* (Charles Scribner's Sons, 1967).

6. See Hiley H. Ward, *Prophet of the Black Nation* (Pilgrim Press, 1969), p. 135.

7. Albert B. Cleage, Jr., *Black Christian Nationalism: New Directions for the Black Church* (William Morrow & Company, Inc., Publishers, 1972), p. 188.

8. See Richard J. Neuhaus, "Liberation Theology and the Captives of Jesus," *Worldview* (June, 1973), pp. 41–48. Cf. Stanley Hauerwas, "Messianic Pacifism," *ibid.*, pp. 29–33.

9. My view has been stated in my *Liberation and Reconciliation*, Ch. VI.

10. John M. Allegro, *The Sacred Mushroom and the Cross* (Doubleday & Co., Inc., 1970).

11. Morton Smith, *The Secret Gospel* (Harper & Row, Publishers, Inc., 1973), pp. 140–141.

12. Henry Nicholson, *Jesus Is Dead* (Vantage Press, Inc., 1971), p. 153.

13. Cone, *A Black Theology of Liberation*, p. 216.

14. Preston Williams, "James Cone and the Problem of a Black Ethic," *Harvard Theological Review*, Vol. LXV, No. 4 (Oct., 1972), p. 484.

15. Oscar Cullmann, *Jesus and the Revolutionaries*, tr. by Gareth Putnam (Harper & Row, Publishers, Inc., 1970).

16. Ernst Käsemann, *Jesus Means Freedom: A Polemical Survey of the New Testament* (Fortress Press, 1970), p. 35.

17. *Ibid.*

18. *Ibid.*, p. 40

19. *Ibid.*, p. 41.

20. Cullmann, *op. cit.*

21. Cone, *A Black Theology of Liberation*, p. 208.

22. Brandon, *op. cit.*, p. xiv.

23. John Howard Yoder, *The Politics of Jesus* (Wm. B. Eerdmans Publishing Company, 1972).

24. Quoted by Stanley Hauerwas, "Messianic Pacifism," *Worldview*, June, 1973, p. 30.

25. *Ibid.*, pp. 30–31.

Chapter 6

THE GOSPEL OF POWER

1. Howard Thurman, *The Luminous Darkness* (Harper & Row, Publishers, Inc., 1965), p. x.

2. Sterling Plumpp, *Black Rituals* (Third World Press, 1972), pp. 48–49.

3. Prentiss Taylor, "Research Liberation: Shaping a New Black Identity in America," *Black World*, Vol. XXII, No. 7 (May, 1973), p. 11.

4. George D. Kelsey, *Social Ethics Among Southern Baptists, 1917–1969* (Scarecrow Press, 1973), p. 13.

5. Samuel S. Hill, Jr., *et al., Religion and the Solid South* (Abingdon Press, 1972), pp. 179–208.

6. Gary T. Marx, *Protest and Prejudice: A Study of Belief in the Black Community* (Harper & Row, Publishers, Inc., 1969), pp. 94–105.

Chapter 7

UNITY WITHOUT UNIFORMITY

1. Michael Novak, "Further Thoughts on Ethnicity," *Christian Century* (Jan. 10, 1973), p. 42.

2. *Ibid.*

3. See James H. Smylie, "Uncle Tom's Cabin Revisited," *loc. cit.*, pp. 72–76.

4. Liston Pope, *Millhands and Preachers: A Study of Gastonia* (Yale University Press, 1942), John C. Bennett makes reference to this study in his *Christian Ethics and Social*

Policy (Charles Scribner's Sons, 1946), p. 98.

5. *Ibid.*

6. Nyerere, *Ujamaa*, p. 11.

7. *Ibid.*, p. 12.

8. Rosemary Ruether, "Sad Songs of Zion," *Journal of Religious Thought*, Vol. XXVIII, No. 2 (1971), pp. 115–116.

9. John Macmurray, *Persons in Relation* (*The Form of the Personal*, Vol. II; London: Faber and Faber, 1961), p. 157.

10. *Ibid.*, p. 119.

11. Shailer Matthews, *Jesus on Social Institutions* (Fortress Press, 1971), p. 52.

12. *Ibid.*, p. 55.

13. The foregoing discussion of I Cor. 12:12–26 has been based in part on *The Interpreter's Bible*, Vol. X (Abingdon-Cokesbury Press, 1953), pp. 160–165.

14. Paul S. Minear, *Images of the Church in the New Testament* (The Westminster Press, 1960), p. 190.

15. *Ibid.*, pp. 190–191.

16. *Ibid.*, p. 192.

17. *Ibid.*, p. 194.

18. William L. Banks, *The Black Church in the United States* (Moody Press, 1972), p. 92.

19. *Ibid.*, pp. 92–93.

20. *Ibid.*, p. 100.

21. *Ibid.*, p. 97.

22. Albert B. Cleage, Jr., *Black Christian Nationalism*, p. xiii.

23. *Ibid.*, p. 60.

24. Cf. Lerone Bennett, "The Challenge of Blackness," *Black Paper No. 1* (April, 1970; Atlanta: Institute of the Black World), p. 2.

25. James Baldwin, "An Open Letter to My Sister, Angela Y. Davis," in Angela Y. Davis *et al.*, *If They Come in the Morning* (The New American Library, Inc., 1971), p. 23.

26. Leon H. Sullivan, *Alternatives to Despair* (Judson Press, 1972), p. 15.

Chapter 8

ETHICS AND ESCHATOLOGY

1. Amos N. Wilder, *Eschatology and Ethics in the Teaching of Jesus,* rev. ed. (Harper & Row, Publishers, Inc., 1950), pp. 11–12.

2. Cone, *A Black Theology of Liberation,* p. 241.

3. *Ibid.,* pp. 245–246.

4. *Ibid.,* p. 247.

5. *Ibid.,* p. 241.

6. *Ibid.,* p. 248.

7. *Ibid.*

8. *Ibid.*

9. *Ibid.* In fairness to Cone, one should consider carefully his essay, "Theological Reflections on Reconciliation," *Christianity and Crisis,* Vol. XXXII, No. 24 (Jan., 1973), pp. 303–308. My observation is that Cone is too close to Barth's theological foundations to lay a good base for a black theological ethic to provide for an action thrust for the black church. Black theology must provide this or it will be stillborn, and time is short. We have not reached our most influential black churchmen with black theology and neither have we moved the black masses who are dutiful churchgoers.

Chapter 9

BLACK THEOLOGY AS POWER

1. Marcel Xhaufflaire, "The Political Theology of J. B. Metz," *Listening,* Vol. VI, No. 2 (Spring, 1971), pp. 109–116.

2. G. Sherwood Eddy, *The Kingdom of God and the American Dream: The Religious and Secular Ideals of American History* (Harper & Brothers, 1941), p. 2.

3. Harvey Cox, "The Churches and the Future of Religion," *Christianity and Crisis,* Vol. XXXIII, No. 1 (Feb. 5, 1973), p. 10.

4. *Ibid.,* p. 11.

5. *Ibid.*

6. Roger Shinn, "Political Theology in the Crossfire," *Journal of Current Social Issues,* Vol. X, No. 2 (Spring, 1972), p. 13.

7. *Ibid.,* pp. 14–16.

8. *Ibid.,* p. 20.

9. Analysis in *Richmond Times-Dispatch,* Jan. 23, 1973.

10. Richard B. Freeman, "Black Income: Delusion and Reality," an editorial, *Washington Post,* July 5, 1973.

11. *Ibid.*

12. *Ibid.*

13. *Washington Post,* July 5, 1973, p. A2.

Chapter 10

LIBERATION AND
RECONCILIATION REVISITED

1. See John J. Carey, "Theologies of Revolution: Hard and Soft," *Anglican Theological Review,* Vol. LIV, No. 3 (July, 1972), pp. 147–161.

2. Buell G. Gallagher, *Color and Conscience: The Irrepressible Conflict* (Harper & Brothers, 1946), p. 3.

3. *Ibid.,* p. 5.

4. Robert W. Terry, *For Whites Only* (Wm. B. Eerdmans Publishing Company, 1970), pp. 17–20.

5. *Ibid.,* p. 41.

6. *Ibid.*

7. *Ibid.,* pp. 20–21.

8. *Ibid.,* pp. 93–97.

9. Harvey Cox, *God's Revolution and Man's Responsibility* (Judson Press, 1969), pp. 103–104.

10. Dietrich Bonhoeffer, *Ethics,* ed. by Eberhard Bethge, tr. by Neville Horton Smith (The Macmillan Company, 1955), p. 71.

11. Cox, *op. cit.,* pp. 46–49.

12. Cf. R. W. Tucker, "Revolutionary Faithfulness," in Marty and Peerman (eds.), *New Theology No. 6* (The Macmillan Company, 1969), pp. 201–206.

13. Jan M. Lochman, *Church in a Marxist Society: A Czechoslovak View* (Harper & Row, Publishers, Inc., 1970), p. 115.

14. *Ibid.,* pp. 115–116.

15. *Ibid.,* p. 115.